D0466481

DIRECTING FOR THE STAGE

DIRECTING FOR THE STAGE

POLLY IRVIN

STAGECRAFT

RotoVision

A RotoVision Book
Published and distributed by RotoVision SA
Route Suisse 9
CH-1295 Mies
Switzerland

RotoVision SA, Sales & Production Office
Sheridan House, 112/116A Western Road
Hove, East Sussex BN3 1DD, UK
Tel: +44 (0)1273 72 72 68
Fax: +44 (0)1273 72 72 69
ISDN: +44 (0)1273 73 40 46
Email: sales@rotovision.com
www.rotovision.com

Copyright © RotoVision SA 2003

All rights reserved. No part of this publication may be
reproduced, stored in a retrieval system or transmitted in
any form or by any means, electronic, mechanical,
photocopying, recording or otherwise, without permission of
the copyright holder.

ISBN 2-88046-661-X
10 9 8 7 6 5 4 3 2 1

Layout by Artmedia Press, London

Production and separations by ProVision Pte. Ltd., Singapore
Tel: +656 334 7720
Fax: +656 334 7721

Although every effort has been made to contact owners of copyright
material which is reproduced in this book, we have not always
been successful. In the event of a copyright query, please contact
the publisher.

CONTENTS

What is the role of director? What exactly is it that they do? How does their work evolve?

In *Directing for the Stage* I have attempted to open the rehearsal room door on some of the greatest directors in the world in order to reveal their directorial secrets.

Directing is a lonely job. Yes, one collaborates with many other artists when producing a piece of theatre but the director is the siphon, the catalyst. The director is the one who walks into the rehearsal each morning with the responsibility of the entire show on their shoulders. It is the director, primarily, who fires the project and it is their vision for the text, actors, design, sound, light and audience experience that is finally realised on the stage. Who can they turn to when it's all crumbling around them, when they lose their confidence? No-one. Because they are the eternal parent. They need to remain always in control, strong and inspired.

One never knows as a director what other directors get up to. Not really. This helps to develop a unique working process but one can't help being curious. For example, I've often been told by actors that working with Declan Donnellan was a turning point in their career, that he taught them to act, that what he does is unlike any director they've ever worked with. I've tried to remain nonchalant at these moments, 'Oh really?' I've replied, but secretly I've longed to stand in the corner of his rehearsal room and observe the genius at work.

This book has given me the opportunity to meet some of the most talented directors in the world and ask them everything I have ever wanted to. Each director was interviewed about their beginnings and the major influences that led them to their working methods, about their approach to rehearsals and how they tackled specific productions. They were asked how they decide what to direct, how they work with actors, and what they think about the future of theatre. Alongside their interviews are illustrations, notes, production photographs and personal photographs which help to illuminate their work.

In producing this book it has been extremely hard to choose just twelve directors from around the globe. Obviously there are omissions. Peter Brook needs to be here, but was unable to participate. As does Arianne Mnouchkine, Peter Sellars, Elizabeth LeCompte, Augustus Boal, Lev Dodin, Silvieu Pucarete and Deborah Warner to name but a few. However, the directors included are from eight different countries, they have all reached the top of their profession and they have all changed the face of that profession in their own special way.

In this book you will find a taster of these directors' unique creative processes. Simon McBurney reveals how he made certain directorial decisions, like how to stage the evocative love-making scene in **The Three Lives of Lucie Cabrol** and talks in depth about his training with Jacques Lecoq. Robert Wilson describes how he directs actors with commands like 'louder', 'faster' 'higher', 'lower'. Anne Bogart reveals her unique collaging technique and describes beautifully the initial tingling effect of a good idea. Declan Donnellan's chapter reveals his own method of unblocking an actor using what he calls 'targeting' and special exercises to release his actors physically and vocally.

Most of these directors have their own company. Anne Bogart was advised to start a company by Arianne Mnouchkine who told her you can't work as a director without one. Lepage has recently formed Ex Machina in Quebec; Donnellan has returned to Cheek By Jowl having experienced working independently; Simon McBurney and Complicite are as one. Eugenio Barba and Habib Tanvir have formed more of a community of people that they have worked with for many years. Others have concentrated on forming strong collaborative relationships such as William Kentridge with Handspring Puppets or Robert Wilson with composers Philip Glass and Tom Waits.

The differences in the role of director change according to their culture, methodology or early influences – or indeed their personality. Some start their process with a script. The directors' primary function then is to interpret that text and to collaborate with designer, technicians and actors in order to successfully translate that text on to the stage. Their task is to enable his or her vision for the play to be realised through the actor's interpretation and visual imagery. Much of the time in rehearsal is spent with the actors exploring the characters' major wants and needs, what Stanislavski calls 'super objectives' that take them through the story from beginning to end or 'objectives' for just one scene or moment. They will help the actor find answers to questions like: where are you?, why are you here?, where have you come from and what are you doing? Some directors will spend a huge amount of time with the text deciphering exactly what the actor is doing to another character when saying each line; this process is known as 'actioning' or finding a characters 'tactics'. Trevor Nunn talks about his process for **The Merchant of Venice** where he spent ten days sitting round a table with his actors working in great depth on the text before starting to work on the floor.

Many other directors in this book work from a completely blank canvas and, together with his or her cast and crew, create a piece of theatre, which both visually and textually has not existed before. Robert Wilson says it's essential to start with an empty space and to get to know that empty space before you put anything in it. Robert Lepage describes having 'peripheral vision'. The great skill is in knowing what you've seen and how to incorporate that into the work. Anne Bogart describes her process as building a table and nailing on a plank at a time to see what it looks like and then trying another angle. Julie Taymor describes finding an ideograph – a broad brush stroke, image or movement containing the essence of a story. There are many variations on these themes and indeed many of our directors choose both text-based and devised methods of working. Eugenio Barba barters theatre in the streets. It's all theatre and it's all directing but the role takes on different guises.

All of these directors are unique. It was, however, their similarities that I found most enlightening. Many expressed a feeling of being an outsider, of not fitting into our merry profession. And in their own way they all decided not to join in but to quietly develop their own work. And it was this work that the world responded to. That is, in itself, what has made them original, where the energy has come from and what keeps them moving forward. They all talk about trusting the process. They all describe a sensation of being open to receiving inspiration from outside of themselves and they all make it sound so easy.

The idea of someone making a career as a theatre director is a relatively new one. Some argue that the role has been taken away from the actor. Irving directed his own company. Burbage was an actor who created his own company. Shakespeare was an actor. Simon McBurney said he thinks the role of a director is enormously overrated and that theatre must belong to the actors because if the actors cannot possess a piece of theatre, it doesn't matter how good the director is. Some directors are accused of doing nothing but casting good actors, which is in itself a great skill. Some directors rely on the designer completely for the setting and staging of a show so that their role becomes more that of coordinator. However, the directors I have interviewed have all explored the possibilities of the role to magnificent extremes and I hope that this book illustrates that the director's role can in itself be that of a great artist.

When I started to work on this book I had just wound down my own theatre company Wild Iris and was in a serious state of flux. What do I do next? Why direct plays? What is theatre? Has it got a future? Who am I doing it for? It was possible that by going to meet some of the greatest practitioners in my field I would be able to answer some of these questions.

The experience has surpassed expectations. I was particularly impressed by their resilience and unending drive and energy. I asked them all if they would ever stop directing and on the whole this was met with guffaws of laughter. Julie Taymor listed a long string of projects that she still wanted to do – more than a lifetime's work. As did Anne Bogart and Trevor Nunn. The problem was not running out of ideas but finding the time to do everything. This was certainly something they all had in common; an undiminishing passion and enthusiasm for their work.

It has been stated by some in recent years that theatre is a dying art form and, with the advent of new technology, film and TV, that theatre is no longer fashionable and therefore has no future. This became my closing question to all the directors that I interviewed. Not all of their answers were included in the final edit but 99 per cent of them said that theatre will never die. The only dissenter was Peter Stein who said, 'of course it will die!' Although he did go on to admit that what he meant was that in its present form it will die. Their belief in the theatre as an inevitable art form is encouraging. Some, like Ninagawa, said that the way forward is to hand theatre back to the actor, to concentrate on the event of live performers in a community. Lepage describes his notion of a theatre where film, technology and live theatre can exist on stage together in a way that has not yet been seen to create a totally new art form. He said he hopes it happens in his lifetime.

All of these directors are extraordinary forces in international theatre. It has been an honour to interview them and an endless source of inspiration. Anne Bogart, in her chapter talks about standing on the shoulders of giants. I have certainly been able to see a great distance standing on the shoulders of all the contributors for this book and I hope that other practitioners, students and theatre enthusiasts can join me from this liberating standpoint where anything seems possible.

I would therefore like to thank all of the directors – Eugenio Barba, Anne Bogart, Declan Donnellan, William Kentridge, Robert Lepage, Simon McBurney, Yukio Ninagawa, Trevor Nunn, Peter Stein, Habib Tanvir, Julie Taymor and Robert Wilson – for giving their time, energy, words, photos and enthusiasm to this book.

A book of this nature is a huge undertaking and relies heavily on the help of many people behind the scenes. People I would like to thank in particular are the directors' personal assistants, general managers and administrators – Rina Skeel, Morag Darby, Jules Cazeddous, Megan Wanlass, Gordan Millar, Sadie Cook, Anita Ashwick, Mark Fedder, Geoffrey Wexler, Yuriko Akishima, Maqry Wafer, Anne McIlleron, Edward Dick, Francine Dupuis, Nathalie Beaulieu, and Aaron Beebe – for their relentless help in pinning the directors down, gathering the visual material and helping us to tie up the many loose ends. I'd like to thank everyone from Rotovision particularly the Commissioning Editor Zara Emerson who approached me in the first place and was the brains behind this series. Also Becky Moss for all her energies pulling this together, Laura Owen for the early stages of research, Nicole Mendelsohn and Amanda Bown for their picture research, Art Editor Luke Herriott, Gary French and Jem Hammond in Production, and everyone else in the office who helped speaking French, German and Japanese to try and track people down. I must also thank Judith Burns at The Home Office for her help and great skill at transcribing, and Chris Taylor for her invaluable help and collaboration at the beginning and for scooping me off the floor at the end. Also Deborah Warner for her support and constant source of inspiration; Annie Castledine for her knowledge and guidance; Simon McBurney again for his invaluable suggestions; all at Rose Bruford, particularly Janet Steel, my colleague on the directing BA, for all the cancelled meetings; Emilio Romero and Antje Diedrich on the European Theatre Arts course for their advice when compiling the list and John Collis in the library for his research material. Great thanks also to Faynia Williams, Sam Jones, Jenny Eldrige, LIFT, BITE, Blanche Marvin, Lucinda Morrison and Mary Parker at the National Theatre Press Office, Jan Ryan, Alby James, Tate Modern, Augusto Boal, Natasha Betteridge and Adjoa Andoh. Most importantly, I want to thank my family, Jon Wilmot, Stanley Irvin Wilmot and Martha Irvin Wilmot for coping with a preoccupied partner and mother; my brother Jim Irvin and friend Sally Still for their journalistic advice and my Mum, Jo Irvin, for always being on the end of the phone and for the foresight to take me to see Peter Brook's **A Midsummer Night's Dream**, aged six. This book is dedicated to my Dad, Lawrence Irvin, for his help and for his talent, imagination and enthusiasm that introduced me to theatre in the first place and showed me the great possibilities of the role of the director.

"I don't need money, I don't need buildings ..."

EUGENIO
BARBA

Eugenio Barba was born in Italy and emigrated to Norway in 1954. After studying theatre in Poland with Jerzy Grotowski, he grew increasingly interested in different theatrical cultures. In 1963, after a six-month tour of India, he published a long essay on Kathakali, a then unknown theatre form in the West. He created Odin Teatret in Oslo in 1964, moving it to Holstebro, Denmark, in 1966 where he converted it into the Nordisk Teaterlaboratorium. In 1979 Barba founded the ISTA (International School of Theatre Anthropology). He is on the advisory board of scholarly journals such as *The Drama Review* and has published many books including *The Paper Canoe* (Routledge) and *26 Letters from Jerzy Grotowski to Eugenio Barba* (Black Mountain Press). Barba has been awarded honorary doctorates from the Universities of Arhus, Ayacucho and Bologna and the Reconnaissance de Mérite Scientifique from the University of Montreal. He is also recipient of the Danish Academy Award, 1980, the Mexican Theatre Critics Prize, 1984, the Pirandello International Prize, 1996, and the Sonning Prize, 2000, from the University of Copenhagen.

1

JUDITH
By Eugenio Barba and
Roberta Carreri
Odin Teatret, Holstebro,
Denmark, 1994

1–3 Roberta Carreri as Judith

2

EUGENIO BARBA: You are always naked and vulnerable when you start your work, just like when you're born, and all the experience of the species doesn't help you. So the methods don't help you. Any one of us who has been doing work as a director or an actor knows that he cannot apply in a direct way the methodology found in books. If we try to emulate a great director like, let's say, Grotowski, the moment we begin to do this we find that the results are not the same and then you have to find the solution yourself. And this is the moment of truth. You are alone. Nobody can help you. When you are in a working space you are in a boat without steering and you go to maps from people who have been doing the navigation before you; but the crew is different, the people you are working with are different. I have nine actors, but with each actor I work in a different way. They have different sensibilities, different ways of being directed. Nevertheless, what we call 'the method' is like an armour which hides something very, very vulnerable, and very seldom are we able to go to the core of it when we read about the experience of the generations who have come before us.

When I began my own company I didn't know what I was doing. I had no experience in teaching, so we had to teach each other. I had been working with the then unknown Grotowski and had gone back to Oslo to get a job. Rightly, the directors couldn't take me seriously. I had no papers, and my only credential was that I had worked with a completely unknown director whose name you couldn't pronounce. So then I had only two possibilities – either to accept what circumstances imposed on me or to say, no, I shatter these circumstances and I shatter them by thinking in a different way. So all right, I couldn't work in a theatre but it would be very easy to work if I was myself a director of a theatre. I said, OK, what do I need first of all? I need human beings. Actors. I don't need money, I don't need buildings, I don't need anything other than human beings, therefore what sort of human beings? Persons who are in the same situation, who want to do theatre and are not allowed to do it. So I went to a theatre school in Oslo, got the list of all the people who had been rejected, contacted them, and exposed the idea of building an avant-garde theatre company. I got from a friend the possibility of working in the evening in a school. It was a very small space but it was enough. Then we began, and after two weeks from 15 people in the beginning, there were only four remaining. I asked my four actors what sort of experience they had. One had been dancing classical ballet as a young bourgeois child, so I said, 'you are the teacher of

3

classical ballet in the group.' Somebody else had been very good at gymnastics in school so then I said, 'you are the teacher of biomechanics and improvisation' – we didn't know what it meant at the time, but it sounded very, very important. So, the fact that we were pupil and teacher, that we were amateur, that we were living in a sort of world of indifference and at the same time we had our personal motivation, gave us a meaning and gave our work an identity. And then the catalyst was the fact that we moved from Norway to Denmark and therefore we had to find other ways to build a dramaturgy because we had no common language with our spectators.

What we were doing at the beginning has now totally disappeared. While training is maybe even more important today than before, it has nothing to do with the beginning. Training in reality means apprenticeship – you are somebody who is trying to integrate into an environment, a trade where you have to function. So in the beginning all this training is in order to make you integrate into this culture which already exists. You have to give up much of your personality in order to integrate and start assuming and accepting certain values or superstitions which are imported. But after a certain period of three or four years you are integrated and you have incorporated the values, and then begins a period where the training goes in a totally different direction; you have to personalise it. It is no longer learning how to function in an environment, it's the opposite. I'm now learning how to make this environment, to shake it. I wouldn't say that it is against this environment, but it is, in a way, autonomous from the environment. And then there is a third period where training in reality has become a sort of 'time space', which is important as a sort of antidote to your own environment. You are not under the pressure of time and the actors are totally free to do what they want. Therefore training becomes a sort of 'personal garden' – as one of my actors, Roberta, says – where you can cultivate just one very special rose. So you see the word 'training' has changed enormously and today training is very much up to the individual. They can gather in twos or threes and start doing certain things together and then after one or two years this material has a sort of consistency. Sometimes they show it to me and then I decide whether to make a production out of it.

For instance, the production I am working on now called **Salt** is a result of training the group has been doing for two-and-a-half years. At first I didn't like the material they showed me

Rooms in the Emperor's Palace toured extensively around South America in 1988. Barba's group have frequently taken their performances to the street to do 'bartering': 'Imagine two very different tribes, each one on their side of the river. Each tribe can live for itself, talk about the other tribe, praise or slander it. But every time one of them rows over to the other side it is to exchange something. One does not row over to carry out ethnographic research, but rather to give and to take. This is the barter.'

1

2

ROOMS IN THE EMPEROR'S PALACE
By Eugenio Barba
Odin Teatret, South America,
1988

1 Richard Fowler and
  Julia Varley
2 The Odin group: Martin
  Damgaard, Tage Larsen,
  Frans Winther, Julia Varley,
  Roberta Carreri, Jan
  Ferslev, Pia Sanderhoff,
  Isabel Ubeda, Pushparajaa
  Sinnathamby, Eugenio
  Barba, Iben Nagel
  Rasmussen, Torgeir
  Wethal, Patricia Alves,
  Rina Skeel, Sigrid Post,
  Kai Bredholt, Ulrik Skeel,
  Louise Andersen
3 Julia Varley as Mr Peanut
4 Julia Varley and
  Kai Bredholt

3

4

ODE TO PROGRESS
By Eugenio Barba
Dedicated to Malika Boussouf
and Susan Sontag
On tour, 1997 to present

1 Kai Bredholt, Torgeir
  Wethal, Tage Larsen
2 Tage Larsen, Jan Ferslev,
  Torgeir Wethal, Iben
  Nagel Rasmussen,
  Roberta Carreri
3 Torgeir Wethal, Iben Nagel
  Rasmussen, Roberta
  Carreri, Tage Larsen,
  Kai Bredholt
4 Kai Bredholt, Jan Feslev,
  Julia Varley and
  Torgeir Wethal
5 (p18 left) Tage Larsen

2   3

but then something happened that made me change my mind. I started thinking that it was time for me to make a testament, because I have arrived at an age where any time one can take the train, or whatever, and one doesn't get off! So I started to think, what is going to happen to this environment? And I understood that I had to leave as much as possible to my actors. So if they had new productions themselves there would be a possibility of keeping them autonomous from a director. We had difficulties in the beginning because I had no idea what to do and then something happened, once again a coincidence. Roberta knows a well-known Italian author, Tabuchi. I knew that Roberta would enjoy performing in Italian, her own language, so I said, 'I want to do this new book of Tabuchi,' and out of this I decided to make **Salt**. I would say that of all the original material the actors presented to me 90 per cent was taken away and replaced with new material which was created in the course of the process.

Very often the material the actors present to me has no such continuity. They can have just certain images and it's very, very short – ten, fifteen minutes or even one or two, a sort of moving or vocal ideogram. It is an agreement here at the Odin that I never ask what the starting point is – they suggest the materials and then I try to find the context. It's very normal that the actor begins with an inner sub-score, an inner action which determines the other actions. I judge the material by how organic it is and also the quality of radiation and suggestive power. I then start to work on two different dramaturgys, one which is the organic dramaturgy of the actors but which is very much rooted in their inner souls, and then the narrative context. Then after this should come a sort of density which is a third element of dramaturgy. One of the qualities I expect an actor to have is to be able to adapt to the tasks which come from the process while trying to keep their inner actions alive. This, in very few schematic words, is the way that we work.

There is a moment in the work where all technique, all your knowledge, disappears and you need to be able to reach this condition of vulnerability. It's so difficult because you are so influenced by your knowledge. Age is horrible not because the body decays but because you are so penetrated, impregnated by habits, knowledge, knowledge, knowledge. I would like to become a five-year-old child who sees the snow for the first time. I have seen so much snow in the world

4

Ode to Progress The story revolves around the mythical 'huldrefolk' – elves, trolls, fairies and gnomes – as they celebrate the transition into the new millenium. The aim of the production was to unite the two worlds of theatre and dance, with the ethos that 'all performance is dance at its physical and mental roots.'

KAOSMOS
By Eugenio Barba
On tour, 1993–1996

(p19) Roberta Carreri and
Eugenio Barba in rehearsal

Kaosmos is inspired by the legend of a man
who doesn't want to die. It tells the story of
a village where, every spring, the villagers
perform 'the ritual of the door', a common
theme in mythology and folklore; a man or
woman asks to be admitted to the Realm of
Happiness or Salvation. A doorkeeper asks
the protagonist to wait. The waiting lasts
a lifetime.

MYTHOS
Based on poems by Henrik
Nordbrandt; adapted by
Odin Teatret
On tour, 1998

1 Poster by Marco Donati
2 Julia Varley as Daedalus

Mythos presents the story of a funeral
wake at the end of the millennium. Around
the corpse of soldier and revolutionary,
Guilhermino Barbosa, are gathered the
characters of Greek myths. They take
possession of him and recount the lies and
horrors that made them eternal. Characters
include Oedipus, Medea, Cassandra,
Orpheus, Icarus, Sisyphus, Odysseus and
here, Daedalus. The narrative explores the
themes of revolution and myth.

Odin Teatret

M Y T H O S

1

in different countries, from Helsinki to Greenland, to the dirty
snow of London streets, so snow is no longer a miracle.
I suppose what keeps me going is a feeling of responsibility
towards my colleagues. Many of them are still of an age of
creativity and possibilities – 45, 50 – it's early. But there's also
responsibility for certain people who depend on what we are
doing. For the majority of people we are not known at all but
in certain spheres we exert a certain influence. In the theatre
you can build an island of freedom, inspite of being excluded,
inspite of being a foreigner in a country full of xenophobia, in
a country where mainstream becomes more and more rigid
in all manifestations – artistic, political, social – so this keeps
me going. Also I still enjoy it, especially when I see the dawn.
Doing a production is like going into a long Scandinavian
winter night. It never ends, you never see the dawn, the
organic doesn't function and the story is banal. But then if you
continue, suddenly you start seeing something very strange,
a darkness which looks like pink and then you go, aha, the
sun is coming, the sun is coming, the spring is coming.

"I'm not an inventor, I steal everything"

ANNE BOGART

Anne Bogart co-founded SITI, The Saratoga International Theatre Institute with Tadashi Suzuki in 1992. Bogart works collaboratively with the company incorporating her systems of stylised movement and visually compelling, non-linear, story-telling. Her productions frequently tour to major international festivals and when the company are not performing they are teaching The Suzuki Method and Viewpoints. Bogart's recent work included a production of Deborah Drattell's **Lilith** at New York City Opera and **Score**, a homage to Leonard Bernstein, at the Humana Festival of New American Plays. She is the recipient of a 2000–2001 Guggenheim Fellowship; 1988 and 1990 Obie Awards; the 1984 New York Dance and Performance (Bessie) Award and the 1980 Villager Award. Bogart is currently a professor at Columbia University, USA, where she oversees the Graduate Directing Program.

ANNE BOGART: I was brought up in a Navy family and every year I'd be put into a brand new school with thousands of new people. Very quickly I found out that there was a place somewhere in each big school where people were making theatre. It was a community that involved love and urgency and short-term romance, and then it was over, which was just like the rest of my life – so it was something that I could believe in and I gravitated towards while still very young. I never acted, but always helped backstage. It wasn't until I was 15 that I saw my first professional theatre – Adrian Hall's production of **Macbeth** – and that was of such extraordinary quality that I decided then and there that for the rest of my life I was going to be a director.

When I eventually began to direct I went to Germany and pretended to be German. I had been inspired by Peter Stein and his company, the Schaubuhne, but it was through some very difficult failures that I realised in fact I couldn't be German – that I actually *am* American – I have an American sense of humour, an American sense of structure, an American rhythm, and that I don't have to be embarrassed about it. My work in the last 20 years has really been about investigating what it means to be an American artist and what our cultural sources are. We pretend we have no history and we actually have an extraordinary history that's very complicated. It's both positive and negative but is a real source of inspiration for me.

I tend to think about projects two years in advance. What happens is always the same thing. It's either in a conversation, or I'm reading something, or I'm on a bus and I get this tingle of excitement – I get a call to adventure from a subject matter or a question which is intriguing to me.

BOBRAUSCHENBERGAMERICA
By Charles L. Mee Jr.
SITI company production
at the Actors Theater of
Louisville, Kentucky, 2001

1–2 Actors rehearsing
3 Anne Bogart
4–5 Actors rehearsing

3

4

5

1

2

SCORE
By Jocelyn Clarke
SITI Company production,
Humana Festival of New
American Plays, USA, 2002

1–2 Tom Nelis as Leonard
     Bernstein

And either that question is already embodied in a play, which I will do, or as a project, which means that I'll find a writer or do it myself and start researching.

For example, years ago *The New York Times* Sunday magazine section had Stephen Hawking on the cover with an article about new physics. It said that the breakthroughs in quantum and astrophysics are so extreme that everyone should study them because it will change the way you understand life. Well, I got that charge of excitement and I went out and bought some novice physics books. The problem was, though, that I found them really hard to understand – I would get to a certain point where an equation would come up and my mind would shut down. So what I did was I got physics books on tape in my car and as I was driving, 10 or 12 hours, I would just let the tape go. I would look at the scenery and the mountains and kind of half listen, and all of a sudden I would get a shock: Oh my God, I just understood, 'Heisenberg's Uncertainty Principle' or 'special relativity'! It was what the physicists call 'fuzzy logic', that if you concentrate too hard on something it disappears, but if you relax your brain accepts it. And then indeed, exactly as the article had said, everything changed for me. My understanding of relationships and life and even stage movement changed because I started understanding these issues found in quantum and astrophysics. But how could I give an audience the same experience I had riding in the car? In other words, how could I give them a landscape to concentrate on while they're listening to these theories?

SMALL LIVES/BIG DREAMS
Devised by the SITI
Company
Originally performed at the
Olympic Festival, Atlanta,
USA, 1994

3 Kelly Maurer

2

ONCE IN A LIFETIME
By Kaufman and Hart
American Repertory Theater,
Massachusetts, USA, 1990

1   Robert Staunton and
    Candy Buckley
2   Mark Zeisler, Candy
    Buckley and Christine
    Estabrook
3   Stephen Skybell and
    Alvin Epstein

I decided to choose a play that involves some of the
principles in physics, a play that everybody knows really well
– **Who's Afraid of Virginia Woolf?** What I did was I got 200
pages of possible text from all these books on physics and
came into rehearsal and gave them to the four actors in my
company. We spent weeks studying them but also staging
Who's Afraid of Virginia Woolf? Eventually, when we had
staged the entire cut-down version, we threw away the Albee
text and replaced every line of dialogue with something
from my 200 pages that was similar in length and rhythm.
What I wanted the audience to do was to give up trying to
understand it very early on and just relax and enjoy the play
they were seeing, and ultimately what they were hearing
would come back and tickle them again. At one point in
rehearsals we got stuck and someone suddenly said, 'the
Bible', so we went to Genesis and Revelations and used lines
from there as well. I know it sounds mad but it was one of
the most moving moments I've had in rehearsal because it
worked so well. That became a show I'm very fond of called
Going, Going, Gone.

People who sit in my rehearsals sometimes say, 'What's Anne
doing? Why are the actors doing all the work?' But that's
actually our process – it's highly collaborative. It's not about
me saying, 'OK, next you go down stage; you go up stage' –
it's never that. We know what we're going after, we have a
structure and we start to work. When we get lost we stop, we
stand in a clump, we figure it out and then we go back to the
work. It's more like building a table: you nail this one board
on and then you go to the next. Sometimes we'll put the table
together and I'll sit and look at it and say, 'Oh my God, why
are there those weird lines? We put those boards on in a
really weird way.' So we'll just get out the hammer and nails,
pull them apart and then put them together again. It's always

3

very practical in terms of physicality – the technicality is always very exact.

We have four company designers. Darren West is the sound designer and he has his digital machinery set up completely from day one. Then the costume designer, James Schette, is in and out of rehearsals, just watching and throwing in suggestions. The set designer, Neil Patel, and I have precious time alone before we begin rehearsal. We come up with a very strong design idea which I bring in on day one and the actors never question it. I feel very strongly about creating a design that's an arena in which certain events can happen, that's open enough for us to invent anything, that's specific enough for us to know exactly how many feet it is from one side to the other. As for the lighting designer, they have not been in the room during rehearsals. They have the strongest dramaturgical minds of anybody – their job is not to just illuminate what I do but to set up an obstacle course in which this thing happens. They have the cleanest, clearest eyes and usually their notes are very hard and very necessary.

When we go into rehearsal, we hit the ground running at top speed. We have three weeks and then tech week before we open. We then spend the next two years refining it while touring sometimes up to four years. **Bob** is going into its fifth year. Some shows are done after three weeks and you really don't have to do a lot of changing; some of them we feel very frustrated with and do major re-changing, taking it back into rehearsal after the initial première.

A show like **Bob** I'm just constantly proud of; I don't feel any pain watching it. When I was a young director I was obsessed with the director, Robert Wilson, so when Bondo – the guy who plays Bob – worked with Wilson one summer I said, 'Look, Bondo, you have to email me every day and tell

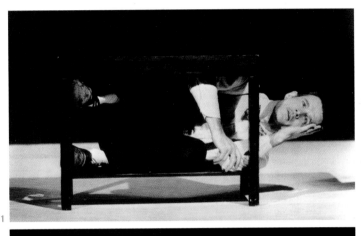

1

2

3

THE MEDIUM
Devised by the SITI Company
Originally performed at the
Toga Festival, Toga, Japan,
1993

1 Tom Nelis

The Medium is based on the
works of Marshal McLuhan, the
story revolving around McLuhan's
passions, ideas, and the convulsions
that eventually led to his death. Tom
Nelis controlled the action with a
remote control.

BOB
Devised by Anne Bogart
and Jocelyn Clarke
SITI Company production
Theatre Archa, Prague, 1998

2 Will Bond

Bob All the words in this production
were spoken by Robert Wilson at
one time or another. However, Bogart
did not intend it to be a realistic
portrait of the great director: 'rather,
a dip into the engaging perspective
about family, art and culture.'

WAR OF THE WORLDS
By Naomi Lizuka
SITI Company production,
2002

3 Stephen Webber and
   Akiko Aizawa

War of the Worlds A piece that
Bogart described as a theatrical
meditation on Orson Welles and his
life, this is the story of a man told in
a kind of dream logic that allows you
to spin backwards and forwards
in time.

Private Lives/Cabin Pressure
Bogart got a grant from the Pugh Foundation for a two-year relationship with the Actors Theater in Louisville, Kentucky. There she pursued her fascination with Noel Coward and decided to direct **Private Lives**. It was during rehearsals of this production that she developed another project. Fifty people from the Louisville area who were not usual theatre-goers were chosen to sit in on a minimum of two rehearsals – one technical rehearsal and one performance. Bogart then interviewed her selected group on the stage after performances in front of the audience that had just seen **Private Lives**. She asked them about their experience of the show and how it differed being in rehearsal. She then transcribed the interviews. Using her extensive research about the actor/audience relationship, she created a text which was to become **Cabin Pressure** – a 'comedy ballet'. Satirising genres from melodrama to Noel Coward, the work examined the love-hate struggle between the theatre-goer and the theatre.

CABIN PRESSURE
Devised by the SITI Company
Originally performed at the
Humana Festival of New
American Plays, USA, 1999

1 Ellen Lauren, Stephen Webber
and Barney O'Hanlon

PRIVATE LIVES
By Noel Coward
Actors Theater of Louisville,
Kentucky, USA, 1998

2 Jefferson Mays and Ellen
Lauren

me what it's like to work with him.' He would email me these hysterically funny stories, and then when we were doing **The Medium** in Dublin and waiting around in tech rehearsals I said, as a joke, 'Bondo, can you *do* Bob?' He got a funny look in his eyes and he walked out of the room and came back into the theatre as Bob. I was laughing so hard I was crying and I said joking, 'Bondo, Bondo, we're going to make a one-man show and it's going to be called "Bob".' At the time, my dear friend Jocelyn Clarke who is a writer in Dublin was there, and he said, 'No, Anne, we *should* do Bob, we should do it.'

Then a few months later my mother was dying and she didn't want me sitting around waiting for her to die. I was very upset and I couldn't sleep at night, so I called my assistant in New York and I said, 'Look, go and get everything Bob ever said in public, go find every article ever written about him and every interview he ever did.' I sat up every night just reading these interviews and highlighting in yellow pen whatever I thought was entertaining and fun and interesting, and then I would type those into my computer. I put them into categories like 'Greetings', 'My Philosophy', 'Gossip' or 'Family'. After I had my 200 pages I sent them to Jocelyn Clarke in Dublin and he stewed on it and sent back a 30-page play called **Bob**.

I'm not an inventor, I steal everything. If I have any talent it's that I can juggle a lot of information at the same time. I use other people's ideas. My inspiration comes from asking, 'whose shoulders am I standing on?' As Isaac Newton said, 'If I can see far it's because I stand on the shoulders of giants.' There are significant reasons why those giants have been forgotten in my country, like the McCarthy era – the kinds of political actions that are so effective that, like Stalinism, you forget them – so my task in life is to remember. To me if theatre was a verb it would be 'to remember' and it's about remembering that you're human and asking, 'What does that mean?'

GOING, GOING, GONE
Devised by the SITI Company
Bernhard Theater, New York,
USA, 1996

3   K. J. Sanchez, Tom Nelis
    and Ellen Lauren

3

Going, Going, Gone Quarks, neutrons and the 'Heisenburg Uncertainty Principle' tango with the Bible, limmericks, *Alice in Wonderland* and the works of Edgar Allen Poe to great effect in this production. Conversations with scientists jostle against snatches of Edward Albee's **Who's Afraid of Virginia Woolf?**

"there's **you,** there's **me** and there's the **space**"

DECLAN DONNELLAN

Declan Donnellan was born in England in 1953 to Irish parents. He read English and Law at Cambridge and was called to the Bar at the Middle Temple in 1979. With designer Nick Ormerod, Donnellan founded Cheek By Jowl in 1981, now widely regarded as one of the world's most influential theatre companies, and has directed the majority of their productions. He introduced British audiences to major and unperformed European classics including **Andromache** by Racine and **Le Cid** by Corneille. From 1989 to 1997 he was Associate Director of the Royal National Theatre. As a freelance director he has worked at the National Theatre of Finland, the Royal Shakespeare Company in the UK, and in 1997 he became the only British director to stage a work with the Maly Theatre Company in St Petersburg, where he directed **The Winter's Tale** in Russian. As a result he received the Christal Tourandot Award, a major award for foreigners who have contributed greatly to Russian culture. He has won several awards in Paris, London, New York and Moscow, including the Olivier Award for Outstanding Achievement in 1991. The following text is an excerpt from his book *The Actor and the Target*, copyright © Declan Donnellan, 2002, published by Nick Hern Books, www.nickhernbooks.co.uk.

DECLAN DONNELLAN: Acting is a mystery, and so is theatre. We assemble in a space and divide into two parts, one of which enacts stories for the remainder. We know of no society where these rituals never happen, and in many cultures these events are at the very centre of that society. There is a persistent need in human societies to witness acted-out representations, from television soap opera to Greek 'tragedy'.

We live by acting roles, be it father, mother, teacher or friend. We construct our sense of self by playing roles we see our parents play, and develop our identities further by copying characters we see played by elder siblings, friends, rivals, teachers, enemies or 'heroes'. Acting is a reflex, a mechanism for development and survival. It isn't 'second nature', it is 'first nature'. 'First nature' cannot be taught; it is not like chemistry or scuba diving, and this primitive instinct to act is the basis of what I mean by 'acting'. So how can we develop or train our ability to act, if acting in itself cannot be 'taught'?

When acting flows, it is alive, and this cannot be analysed; but problems in acting are connected to structure and control, and these can be usefully analysed. Rather than claim that 'x' is a more talented actor than 'y', it is more accurate to say that 'x' is less blocked than 'y'. The 'talent' is already pumping away, like the circulation of the blood. We just have to dissolve the clot. Removing things isn't always negative; what could be more positive than the surgeon teasing out the tumour? The surgeon can't make life; but he can try to stop life being stopped. Getting rid of things may be inspired: it is said that Michelangelo, when asked how he imagined the statue, replied that he just looked into the marble and chiselled away what 'shouldn't be there'.

Whenever actors feel blocked the symptoms are remarkably similar, whatever the country, whatever the context.

1

2

Boris Godunov Donnellan has worked
extensively in Russia, in both St Petersburg
and Moscow, and his book *The Actor and the
Target* was originally published in Russian.
As Associate Director of the Russian Theatre
Confederation he directed **Boris Godunov** in
2001 and is about to embark on a programme
of work starting with a production of **Twelfth
Night** which will première in Moscow in 2003.

BORIS GODUNOV
By A. Pushkin
Designed by Nick Ormorod
Originally performed at
Moscow Arts Gorky Theatre,
2001

1 Yevgeny Mironov as
  Grigory Otrepev
2 Yevgeny Mironov as
  Grigory Otrepev and
  Irina Grineva as
  Marina Minishek

3

Le Cid This was the first production of the
play at Avignon since the version with Gérard
Philippe in 1947. The new production was
unanimously hailed by the French press and
was invited to perform in Madrid, Rome
Moscow, New York and London.

LE CID
By Corneille
Avignon Festival, France,
1986

1 Michelle Bauman as
  Don Diegue and William
  Nadylam as Rodrigue

DECLAN DONNELLAN

1

2

HOMEBODY/KABUL
By Tony Kushner
Cheek By Jowl and The Young
Vic in association with New York
Theatre Workshop
The Young Vic Theatre, London,
2002

1 Nadim Sawalha,
   Jacqueline Defferary
   and Silas Carson
2 Silas Carson and
   Nadim Sawalha
3 Nadim Sawalha and
   Jacqueline Defferary
4 Souad Faress, Silas Carson,
   Nadim Sawalha and
   Jacqueline Defferary
5 Mark Bazeley and
   William Chubb

4

5

Homebody/Kabul Donnellan first directed
Tony Kushner's play, set in 1998, at the New
York Theatre Workshop in the Autumn of
2001. Casting and preparation were both well
underway when the terrorist attacks on New
York occurred. Rehearsals took place through
that Autumn a few blocks from Ground Zero
with the air still polluted from the catastrophe.
Kushner and Donnellan remounted the play
with Cheek By Jowl in London and Barcelona
the following year.

3

Sometimes the actor feels sluggish and lost; occasionally, the actor starts to feel exposed, with an underlying sense of judgement emanating from outside and within. Two aspects of this state seem particularly deadly: the first is that the more the actor tries to force, squeeze, and push out of this cul-de-sac, the worse it seems to get. Second is the accompanying sense of isolation. As it gets worse, the problem can be projected out, and 'it' becomes the 'fault' of script, or partner, or shoes. But two basic symptoms remain the same, namely paralysis and isolation – an inner looking and an outer locking. This can result in an immobility from eye to brain to heart to lung to lips to limbs, and an overwhelming sense of being alone, a creeping sense of being both responsible and powerless, unworthy and angry, too small, too big, too cautious, too, too, too... 'me'.

'I don't know what I'm doing.' This is the mantra of the blocked actor and can prise open a trap through which everyone in the rehearsal can tumble. The structure of the statement is important. The word 'I' is repeated. The cry implies that: 'I can, should, must, ought to know what I am doing; even that it is my right to know what I am doing which I am somehow being denied.' But this reasonable sounding complaint has entirely ignored something crucial. It is crucial to see that the demands of 'know' and 'I' cannot be resolved unless we deal with the nameless one first. So we will start with the 'something', so neglected that it hasn't yet even been given a name. The nameless one I will call 'the target'.

You cannot ever know what you are doing – full stop. That is, you can never know what you are doing until you first know what you are doing it to. For the actor, all 'doing' has to be done to something. The actor can do nothing without the target. The target can be real or imaginary, concrete or abstract. The target can in fact be anything, but the unbreakable first rule is that at all times and without a single exception there must be a target. For example; 'I impress Juliet', 'I warn Romeo', 'I deceive Lady Capulet', 'I open the window', 'I remember my family'. It can also be 'yourself', as in 'I reassure myself'. All an actor can play are verbs, and each of these verbs has to have a target after it. This target is a kind of object, either direct or indirect, a concrete thing seen or sensed, and needed. There is plenty of choice within the rule of the target. What the target may actually be will change from moment to moment. But without the target the actor can do absolutely nothing at all. The target is the source of all the actor's 'life'.

2

The Winter's Tale The Maly Theatre and Cheek By Jowl have performed in the same festivals since 1986. In 1997 Lev Dodin invited Donnellan and designer Nick Ormerod to stage a production for the St Petersburg actors that they had come to know so well. The result was **The Winter's Tale** which won the Golden Mask in Moscow and is still running in St Petersburg.

THE WINTER'S TALE
By William Shakespeare
Maly Theatre, Cheek By Jowl,
St Petersburg, Russia, 2002

1 Centre: Piotr Semak
   as Leontes

2 Nick Ormerod, designer,
   with Declan Donnellan
   in rehearsal for **Fuente
   Ovejuna** at the National
   Theatre in London

Lady Betty Donnellan's family comes from Roscommon in West Ireland, and **Lady Betty** was inspired by a local legend of a mad woman who murdered her own son and was incarcerated by the British in Roscommon jail as a female executioner. The production incorporated both Irish dance and music specially written by Paddy Cunneen.

LADY BETTY
Written by Declan Donnellan
Cheek By Jowl, Almeida
Theatre, London, UK, 1988

1 Sally Dexter as Lady Betty

When actors feel blocked, when actors feel that they 'don't know what they are doing', it is normally because they do not see the target. The danger is extreme, because the target is the only source of all practical energy for the actor. Without food we die. All life needs to take something from outside itself to inside itself to survive. Actors are nourished and energised by what they see in the world outside. In fact, the very word theatre comes from the Greek 'theatron', which means 'a place for seeing'. Seeing is often used as a metaphor to describe all our contact with the outside world, and the sighted appear to fear blindness more than loss of any other sense. The blinding of Gloucester may appal, but there exists a fate grimmer than having your eyes torn out. That is the punishment inflicted on Oedipus: self-inflicted

1

1

THE DUCHESS OF MALFI
By John Webster
Originally performed at
Wyndhams Theatre,
London, UK, 1995
Designed by Nick Ormerod

1 Anatasia Hille as the
   Duchess and George
   Anton as Bosola

The Duchess of Malfi This was Cheek By
Jowl's first production of a play by Webster.
The production marked the company's debut
in Buenos Aires.

blindness. Sadly this is not such an exotic affliction; blinding ourselves is the cause of block.

We cannot force ourselves to see. We can manipulate ourselves not to see, and are expert at that. We can only force ourselves to 'look at' things. But 'looking at' is quite different from 'seeing'. The distance between 'seeing' and 'looking at' is crucial for the actor. 'Seeing' is about being free enough to pay attention to what already exists. 'Looking at' is more safely about me, more reassuringly about concentration, which we can turn on and off like a tap. Concentration seems so safe; but it isn't. We choose concentration above attention because we can make concentration. Attention is different. It is given and has to be found. We excrete concentration by the cartload and think we can control its coming and going. That's precisely why it's not much use. We cannot control attention, that's why it is so useful, and so frightening. It seems so safe at home, it seems so frightening on the streets, but this is a delusion.

For the actor, 'seeing' is going outside. This active target locates the energy outside so that we can live off it; the target becomes an external battery. Instead of always wondering 'What am I doing?' it is more helpful for the actor to ask 'What is the target making me do?' or: 'What is my partner doing to me?' Again: 'Why do I love Orlando?' is not as helpful as 'What would I have to do if this man made me "love him"?'

We have considered that, for the actor, we are only what we see. If, then, the target is so important, how do we get cut off from it? The answer is simple. Fear cuts us off from the target. Fear severs us from our only source of energy; that is how fear starves us. No theatre work absorbs more energy than dealing with the effects of fear; and fear is, without a single exception, destructive. The more fear stalks the rehearsal room, the more the work suffers. For example, fear makes it difficult to voice conflict. Fear makes it difficult to disagree. Fear creates as much false consensus as false strife. A healthy working atmosphere, where we can risk and fail, is indispensable. Fear corrodes this trust, undermines our confidence and clots 'our work'.

I use an exercise I call the 'message exercise' to help actors lose this sense of paralysis and inner looking. The idea is to get them away from the text and to respond to what they see. I give the actors the words 'there's you, there's me and there's the space'. This is the message. The rule of the exercise is that the words of the message can in no way be altered. For example, the actress playing Juliet must repeat these words to Romeo who uses the same message, and they must play the scene for all it is worth. The actors will get frustrated, as the text is so banal, but that frustration will push them into using their bodies and imaginations to express themselves. They will point, gesture, use different vocal pitches, run, or whisper. When the actress has lost herself in what she is trying to do I will shout 'text!' and the actress will launch without thinking into Shakespeare's text. After a few tries that physical freedom discovered through the banality of the message will start to appear in the 'text of Shakespeare'.

When we make theatre we tell stories. Each time we tell a story it is different; the ancient myth changes each time we hear it. Even if we stick to precisely the same words and intonations, like an Irish bard with his harp, each retelling unfolds the heroic exploits with slight differences. The story changes because the tellers and hearers change, time changes. It is one thing to tell a story, another to define what the story means. When we try to control all the meanings of a story we invariably fail. An advertisement on behalf of a politician can actually convince us not to vote for his weak smile. Manipulation can reverse its 'desired effect'.

The wise actor learns not to try to control what the audience sees. The target needs to be discovered and seen, that is all. The target generates the impulse to act. What the actor plays springs from seeing the target and not from the character's inner will. The shape of the scene is living and mobile; its form is determined by the shifting nature of the targets. The wind shapes the sand; the sand does not shape 'itself alone'.

The actors sees for us: things we want to see and also things that we don't want to see. The infant millenium is screaming: the actor's capacity to see the target in all its messy ambivalence has never been more precious.

1

Fuente Ovejuna For Donnellan's first production as Associate Director of the Royal National Theatre, designer Nick Ormerod bisected the stage with a long traverse to provide a space for processions and ritual. As usual, Donnellan collaborated with director of movement Jane Gibson and musical director Paddy Cunneen. The production was invited to represent the UK at Expo '92 in Seville, where it received an unusual ovation on the first performance, when the local audience burst into spontaneous flamenco.

FUENTE OVEJUNA
By Lope de Vega; adapted by Adrian Mitchell
Royal National Theatre, London, UK, 1992

1 Pamela Nomvete as Pascuala and Rachel Joyce as Laurencia

ANGELS IN AMERICA PART 1: MILLENNIUM APPROACHES
By Tony Kushner
Cottesloe Theatre, London, UK, 1992

2 Nancy Crane as the angel

Angels in America marked Donnellan's first collaboration with Tony Kushner. This six-hour epic on politics, AIDS and redemption established Tony Kushner as a major playwright.

"I understood that **theatre** could be a branch of **drawing**"

WILLIAM KENTRIDGE

The work of South African artist William Kentridge meshes the personal and the political in an innovative use of charcoal drawing, animation, film and theatre. His work presents a nuanced view of current South African society and the fraught legacy of apartheid – from the hearings of the Truth and Reconciliation Commission to the traces of violence registered in the landscape around Johannesburg. Kentridge constructs animated films using a technique he has termed 'stone-age filmmaking'; each sequence goes through a process of successive alteration, erasure, and overdrawing to a single drawing at the end of the process. Since 1992 his theatre work has been in collaboration with Handspring Puppet Company, creating multimedia pieces using puppets, live actors and animation. Kentridge nonetheless sees his artistic production, whether films, theatre, or printmaking, as rooted in drawing. He attracted international critical attention in 1997, when his work was featured in Documenta X in Kassel; 2002 saw him back in Kassel for Documenta XI, staging his most recent theatre production. 2001 saw the launch of a show of Kentridge's work at the Hirshhorn Museum in Washington.

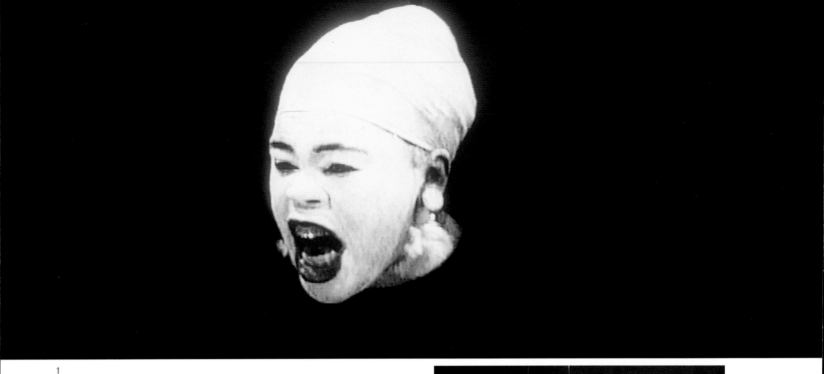

1

Ubu and the Truth Commission was
the result of colliding documentary material
from South Africa's Truth and Reconciliation
Commission (TRC) and Alfred Jarry's
bombastic tyrant Ubu; the sober text of the
TRC was used to give substance to the
burlesque of Ubu, to give a form to the
documentary material. The play began as
a series of etchings, each representing a
possible scene from an unwritten,
unperformed Ubu play. Only when the series
of etchings was complete did the idea of
working towards an Ubu theatre piece take
shape. Initially the theatre piece was going to
be a duet between a dancer on stage and
animated chalk drawings on screen.

2

WILLIAM KENTRIDGE: For years I did both drawing and theatre, approaching them from different angles – the drawing started from nothing; the theatre started from a script. I left theatre for ten years and only came back when I understood that theatre could be a branch of drawing. When you start a drawing there are a few broad strokes somewhere in the middle and gradually a shape is found, and in the activity of making it you find what it's going to be. This is natural, but it's not the normal way of working when making a piece of theatre.

My re-entry into theatre came out of a combination of me seeing some of the productions of the South African-based Handspring Puppet Company, and their seeing the animated films I'd made. We said, 'what happens if we put these together?' There's a kind of parity between the carved wood in puppet theatre and the drawn world of animation (puppets are a kind of three-dimensional drawing). That was the starting point.

When working with puppets, I often start somewhere in the middle of a piece with an image or one particular puppet, and from that I work outwards – even to the extent of saying, 'we have this landscape, this puppet – what is the story they're going to perform?' That is how we arrived at **Woyzeck**. We had a series of characters and landscapes, and we thought, should we do **Carmen** or **Faust**? In the end the one that worked best was **Woyzeck** – partly because it had short scenes so could accommodate the limitations of carrying puppets (any longer than four minutes at a time becomes a problem for the manipulators). There are a series of considerations outside the theme that determine the piece of theatre we do. The first production we did used large puppets and the manipulators were visible. We spent weeks trying to hide them – putting them in black coats, putting boards just above them so they would be in shadow while the puppets were held out in the light. It took a long time to understand the fact that seeing the manipulators was a vital part of the performance.

The puppets often inform the material we are working with; their limitations determine how we operate and also the meaning we are making. For example, in **Ubu and the Truth Commission**, I wanted a pack of dogs. Adrian Kohler, the puppet maker, started by making them from household objects, and they looked fine as sculptures but looked like

UBU AND THE TRUTH COMMISSION
By Jane Taylor
Multimedia puppet theatre collaboration with Handspring Theatre Company
Originally performed at Kunstfest, Weimar, Germany, 1996

1 Busi Zokufa
2 Drawing for the animation: chalk and pastel on black paper
3 Dawid Minnaar and Adrian Kohler in the stage performance

1   2   3   4

Ubu Tells the Truth Kentridge's work frequently crosses over from directing to film-making to his own personal explorations in other media of the subjects that inspire him. The etchings (1–4) on this page are for the animation **Ubu Tells the Truth**. The crocodile-handbag puppet eating the 'evidence' is from the theatre production of the same theme **Ubu and the Truth Commision** (5).

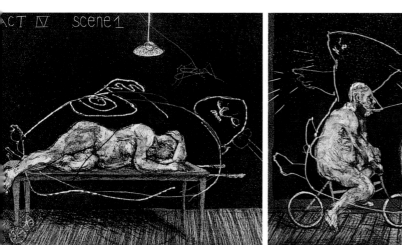

nothing on stage. Then Adrian decided we needed two manipulators for each dog, which suddenly meant we needed six manipulators just for the three dogs – and then we still needed someone for Ubu and Ubu's wife. Our cast was five, so that was already out of the question. We had to consolidate; we said, 'all right, instead of having two manipulators per puppet why don't we put all three dogs into one puppet so it becomes a kind of three-headed dog?' We ended up with the three dogs' heads attached to a suitcase so only three manipulators were needed. The character of the three-headed dog – three different characters reluctantly sharing one fate – became part of the heart of the material of the play. What started its life as a kind of technical concern, or as a limitation, became a character in its own right and carried with it a whole weight of associations.

This play had to do with the evidence that came out in the Truth and Reconciliation Commission in South Africa. It was said at the time that there was a battle between the photostat machines and the paper shredders – for each police officer shredding evidence there were junior officers photostatting it to keep as insurance. We wanted to have some way of showing this. First we thought of having an actual paper shredder on stage and then we thought of a bread-slicing machine shredding loaves of bread continuously. However, the stage managers raised an objection to cleaning it up and anyway it seemed a little too cerebral. Eventually we decided that Ma Ubu would have a pet crocodile with a huge jaw. The crocodile was then attached to her handbag into which she could feed all the past evidence.

The start of the process is almost always some weeks of drawing. In the case of **Confessions** I started by tearing jointed black silhouette shapes such as I had used in one of my films, *Shadow Procession*. I wanted a simple animation, and at first I thought they would be manipulated and filmed frame by frame, and this film projected as an element of the theatre piece. The starting point was making some of these silhouette figures. The next stage was talking to a South African composer, Kevin Volans, and a writer, Jane Taylor, who had written the **Ubu** script. Having made these torn-out shadow puppets I enlisted Handspring Puppet Company to see if it were possible to make the large silhouette figures on a human scale, to be worn by the actors. In addition to making these, Adrian Kohler made some small puppet figures from the torn paper cut-outs – mounted on sticks so

IL RITORNO D'ULISSE
Multimedia opera in collaboration with Handspring Puppet Company
Originally performed at kunstenFESTIVALdesarts, Brussels, Belgium, 1998

1 Basil Jones, Scot Weir
2 Drawing for animation, charcoal on paper
3 Drawing for animation, charcoal and pastel on paper

2

3

Il Ritorno d'Ulisse The principle of the work with the Handspring Puppet Company has been the movement of the performance from the actor through the puppet to the audience. The actor focuses on the puppet, and the puppet is open to the audience. In this production the singers focused on the puppets and each character is made up by the duality of the performance of the actor or singer and the puppet.

1

Confessions of Zeno Shadow puppets have formed a small part of earlier productions with the Handspring Puppet Company, but came to the centre of the performance in **Zeno at 4am** and **Confessions of Zeno**. The form of the shadow puppets plus string quartet plus actor was primary. Jane Taylor's adaptation of Italo Svevo's *Confessions of Zeno* was grafted onto this form.

they could be operated in real time and not simply animated under a camera. We had an evening when Kevin played chords on the piano to see what his minimalist music would do with these figures; Adrian walked one figure slowly across the back of a sofa, and 80 per cent of the work was done. We knew the language, we knew the kind of music, and we had a sense of the theme. We worked outwards from there.

In the rehearsal room we have a track set up in which we can slide drawings behind the shadow puppets – like a toy theatre. In front of the puppets there's a roll of acetate on which there are black ink drawings. In part 2 of **Confessions of Zeno**, Zeno talks about the four sisters – Ada, Alberta, Anna and Augusta – and it's about his courtship of one and marrying of another. We have a sense of these four silhouette women being able to turn into chairs as they change their angle, so the quartet are singing both as women and also as chairs. We have the possibility of things on the front acetate moving, and of the drawings at the back shifting from a bourgeois room to a much more abstract, neutral space. We have a string quartet, Zeno and two women singers on stage.

2

CONFESSIONS OF ZENO
Based on the novel by
Italo Svevo
Multimedia shadow oratorio
in collaboration with
Handspring Puppet Company.
Originally performed at
kunstenFESTIVALdesarts,
Brussels, Belgium, 2002

1 Drawing and
   shadow puppet
2 Dawid Minnaar
3 Ledger-book drawing
   (sketch for costume
   designs); charcoal on
   found pages
4 Drawing for animation;
   charcoal on paper

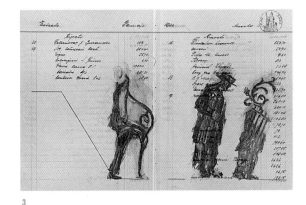

3

4

That's the raw material. The heart of the work is testing the different combinations and seeing what emerges – what we recognise in front of us. What is the meaning if the actors in the front of the stage are primary and the shadows are secondary? What is the meaning if an image on the screen affects the performance in front of it? There is a huge reliance on recognition, on the stage in front of us; and a suspicion of ideas worked out in the abstract. It is a very practical activity. The ideas and meaning follow what we see on stage rather than precede it. The second half of the rehearsal involves extremely rigorous drilling. It is very counter-intuitive; for example, we may try to get a shadow puppet to exit walking, checking that the two legs aren't sliding but moving on an imaginary ground plane. It takes a lot of practising and looking and co-ordinating. There is a whole sidestage choreography: 'You pick up this puppet and give it to me because after I've finished it goes to that person and I've got to run round with it.' It's not like, 'this is my character and how do I keep the psychology in it?' So a lot of my work has to be about making everything precise, getting the manipulation accurate.

The character of Zeno is a hard part for the main actor. It's very much about Zeno not having a voice. He has a spoken voice but the main voices are his father, a bass, and his wife and his mistress, who are both sopranos. And there's a whole load of stuff on the screen to interact with. One piece of animation shows a panther striding backwards and forwards. In one sense it's half mirroring Zeno moving from his wife to his mistress and back again, but it's much more about being in a chronic state of indecision. If the actor simply walks backwards and forwards at his pace ignoring the screen, there's a strange rhythm with the animal going slightly faster and catching up and passing him. It feels kind of idiotic for the actor, because he feels there's nothing happening: 'I'm just walking backwards and forwards!' In fact, there's a whole drama happening with the panther representing the actor's thoughts catching up and bypassing him on the screen. There's a lot of work in terms of giving the actor confidence in what else is happening on stage.

I go through a cycle – it's a kind of rhythm – after working on a theatre project it's fantastic to have a year in my studio on my own without anyone else about. But after a year on my own in my studio it's good to have ten other people to work with. It's a rhythm I really work hard to keep.

1

2

FAUSTUS IN AFRICA!
Based on Goethe's *Faust*
with additional text by
Lesego Rampolokeng
Multimedia puppet theatre
collaboration with Handspring
Puppet Company
Originally performed at
Kunstfest, Weimar,
Germany, 1995

1/3 Drawings for animation;
    charcoal and pastel
    on paper
2   The puppets
4   (pp58–59) Busi Zokufa,
    Dawid Minnaar,
    Adrian Kohler

Faustus in Africa! This play takes part
1 and part 2 of Goethe's *Faust* and sets
them in colonial Africa. The starting
point of the production was a rebuttal of
Hegel's dictum, 'after the pyramids World
Spirit leaves Africa, never to return' –
a view of Africa popular in Europe in
the 18th century, and again now.

3

4

Faustus in Africa! A 'double' Faustus caught
between Gretchen and Helen.

"As a **director** you need to have **peripheral** vision ..."

ROBERT LEPAGE

Born in 1957, Robert Lepage trained at the *Conservatoire d'art dramatique de Quebec* and at Alain Knapp's theatre school in Paris. In 1980 he returned to Quebec and started working on the fringe scene where he began to develop his own devising skills before joining Jacques Lessard's Théâtre Repère. He was introduced to the RSVP cycles which Lessard had picked up from Anna and Lawrence Halprin's San Francisco Dancers' Workshop and incorporated this into his own working methods. His one-man show **Vinci**, 1986, won Avignon's Coup de Pouce prize but it was his six-hour **La Trilogy des Dragons** (The Dragons Trilogy) which really began to mark his reputation. His unique style of ingenious non-linear story telling, bi-lingualism and his multimedia work often explores big subjects of life and the universe, weaved seamlessly with domestic ordinariness.

ROBERT LEPAGE: In Quebec City in the sixties and seventies theatre was a mundane activity, something for the bourgeoisie. When the school took us to see **Twelfth Night** I thought it was the director who was playful, not Shakespeare, because he was old. Of course, with time, I discovered that Shakespeare *was* playful and playfulness became an important element of my work. Then there was rock 'n' roll, Genesis and Jethro Tull and all these guys with weird costumes who played characters and told stories – they really influenced me.

I had a difficult training as an actor because I had this passion for staging and writing and set designing and, you know, doing everything you don't do if you're supposed to be a serious actor. So when I left theatre school, I felt very free and started a little theatre company. People got really interested in what we were doing but we weren't business men; we didn't know how to ask for a grant, we didn't know anything – we were 20 years old. So we joined up with Jacques Lessard. His company had lost its grant and he gave us his last 50 bucks to devise a cafe-theatre show. There were three suitcases and a big Japanese shumi drawing – that was it. It was a huge hit.

Quebec is my home and it's a very alive and vibrant society, but it's also very isolated. I could see all these choreographers, much younger than me, travelling and coming back connected to what was going on in the world. The theatre people were 50 years behind and I wondered why. I decided it was because of language so I said, 'well, what we do is visual, so it shouldn't be a problem,' and we began touring **The Dragons Trilogy** all over the world.

One thing I've always done is start rehearsals with a map. The company draw and draw and eventually these drawings reveal something about the show. When I started **A Midsummer Night's Dream** at the Royal National Theatre, London, I had absolutely no concept, so we did a workshop. We had this big piece of paper and the actors had to draw their dreams. The first day is just trying to find the right colour marker, but with time a map appears. People put all the trees in one area – you have the forest; somebody dreams he was drowning in a lake – so you have this big lake. Eventually this drawing becomes this very logical map of the subconscious. Drawing and using images is a good way of finding people's inner visions. It's a different way of looking and eventually the

The Far Side of the Moon, a show themed on space travel and Buzz Aldrin, became a personal homage to Lepage's mother who had died during the show's development period. One of the physical elements that brought these themes together was a large washing machine that Lepage had found in a skip. It evoked simultaneous memories of his childhood, when his mother took him to the laundromat, and space travel through a child's imagination.

THE FAR SIDE OF THE MOON
By Robert Lepage

1–3 Robert Lepage

1

2

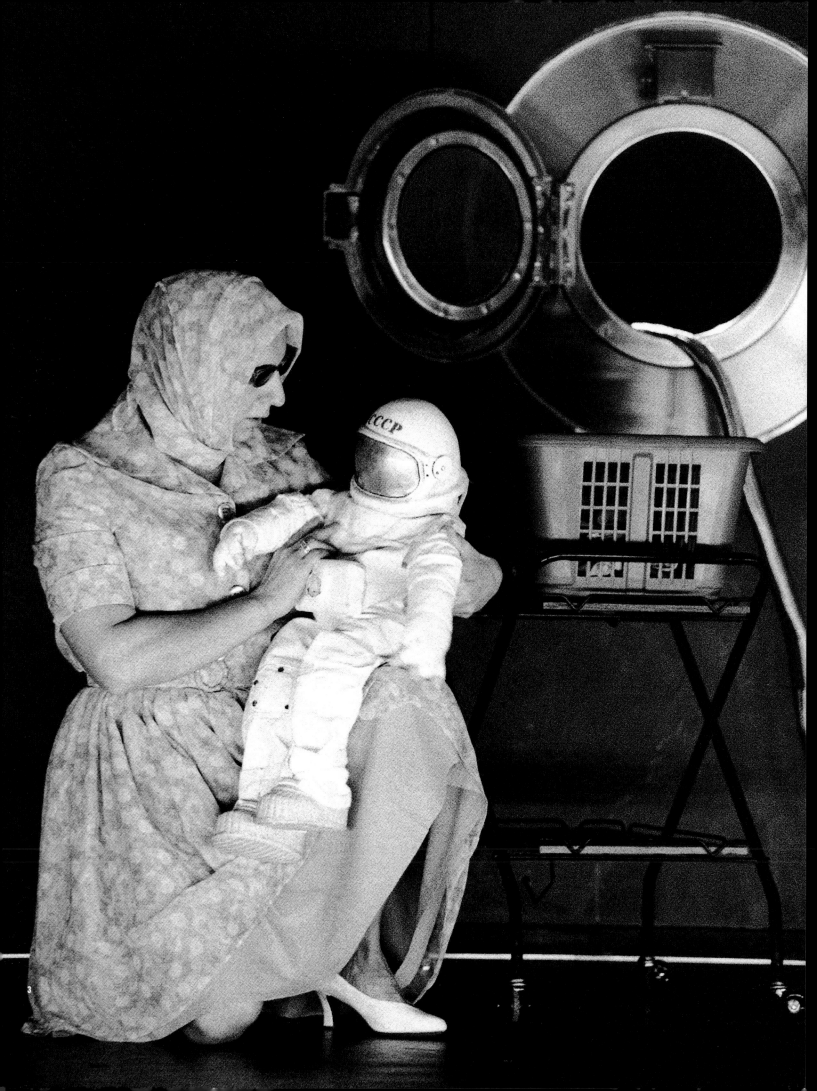

1

Shakespeare Cycle:
Macbeth/Coriolanus/The Tempest
Here, Lepage was able to explore three of
the classic Shakespearean genres (tragedy,
metaphysical comedy and epic drama).
He brought together local actors and
actresses to experiment with the concept
of the 'permanent troupe'. This method of
simultaneously staging several plays over
a prolonged period gave the cast a unique
opportunity to examine the author's work by
taking on a number of different roles. Lepage
was also inspired by Michel Garneau's
forceful and poetic translation, as he
recognised his own passion for language.
The troupe dedicated themselves to
Garneau's texts, comparing them to the
original works, and to translations by
Hugo, as well as Japanese and German
translations. This study brought them closer
to the heart of Shakespeare's plays, thus
helping enrich their performances.

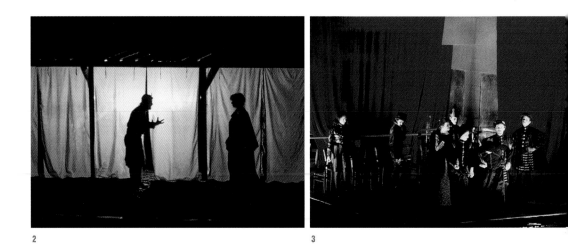

2   3

map looks like the group, and it becomes very clear because you've been in contact with the inner fibres of what you're trying to weave.

So then the designer and I looked at the drawings and we saw mud, mud and water, water and mud, and the eye of the moon looking down. So he said, 'well, let's do it in mud', and we started playing with the idea. Meanwhile Patsy Rosenburg, the voice coach, goes to the parish records in Stratford to see if there's any kind of connection with something that happened when **A Midsummer Night's Dream** was written and finds out that it had rained non-stop for a year. If you read the parish records it's Titania's speech when she says to Oberon, 'because of our quarrels the world is upside down and it's raining and the crops are rotting and animals are desperate and fallen in the mud.' She says the word 'mud' three or four times. It was magical, as it confirmed we were going in the right direction.

As a director you need to have peripheral vision, and for that to happen you have to have visited every corner. In **The Far Side of the Moon** we were sitting around the table, having this very intense discussion about what the show is about. We'd been playing with reflections from a big mirror that kept flopping forwards and showing the floor and we're talking about anti-gravity and all these big concepts because the show is about the Russian Space Programme. Out of the corner of my eye I see a technician just kind of rolling some duct tape across the floor – as it rolls past the mirror it looks like it's floating in mid-air. That became the final scene of the show. I rolled on the floor and the reflection in the mirror looked like I was floating in space.

There's a moment where these things meet in these accidents but you have to have the patience to let that happen, to wait for them. You have to put yourself in an environment where you just kind of throw things, create chaos if you want some kind of order to find its way. To do this in **The Far Side of the Moon** we spread seven weeks of rehearsals over six months. The very first week we just toyed with the idea, did improvisation, played with new gadgets, but nothing was related. Then a month goes by and everybody comes back for a second two-week period but now they're connected to the theme; they've seen things, read an article, or found a book, and I've asked for some things to be constructed like a set of sliding doors. They

4

5

SHAKESPEARE CYCLE: MACBETH/ CORIOLANUS/THE TEMPEST
By William Shakespeare; translated and adapted by Michel Garneau
Co-production with Théâtre Repère, Quebec, Théâtre du Manège, Maubeuge, Theater am Turm, Frankfurt and Zürcher Theater Spektakel, Zürich
First performed at the Théâtre du Manège, 1992

1   **Coriolanus** with Marie Brassard and Anne-Marie Cadieux
2   **Macbeth**
3–5 **The Tempest**

1

came about because I was torn between two ideas – a show about space and the moon and Buzz Aldrin, but also my mother had just died and I wanted to talk about that too. Then, completely by chance, I found this washing machine in the garbage. It was just there, and I remembered when my mother took us to the laundromat; all those great machines – they were space-travel machines. My two ideas connected, so I played with this thing, this image. I wanted to go through its door and I wanted to project on it, so this machine got screwed upright onto a big board but then we needed to get rid of it. So, in the next rehearsal session, a month later, we had sliding doors. That's how the set was developed; we played with the idea and we had it constructed. It's never something that you think about – I never sit down and squeeze ideas out of myself. No, the material is just there. It's how you look at it – that's where the show is.

What I find fantastic is that you can't tell who brought what to the process. I would do an improvisation and the technicians would open their Powerbooks, get on the web and be finding out about cosmonauts and weather-map images. They were

feeding me stuff I'd be playing with all the time. Technicians have to be in the rehearsal room. When we did **Seven Streams of the River Ota**, they were all there from day one and the show became a huge, creative collective. We don't present it to them that way, we don't make it official – we just let it happen.

To provide and explore all these things I have a centre in Quebec City, called La Caserne. It's a very simple place even though its fairly high tech, but ideal for international co-productions, and nowadays I will only do a project on the condition that Ex Machina, our company, is the producer. You see, we will do something that cannot be done in most buildings, because there they have to deal with unions and craftsmen who don't play with technology. But the real deal for me is that we have the room to explore. We do stuff they could never, ever do in a three-week rehearsal – we bring in acrobats and dancers, we bring acoustic specialists, specialists of high-definition TV, whatever. We get the right people. Everybody who has any kind of artistic input is walking around, trying things, and it's very inspiring. The

A MIDSUMMER NIGHT'S DREAM
By William Shakespeare
Royal National Theatre,
London, UK, 1992

1 Oberon and the fairies
2 Angela Laurier as Puck
and Timothy Spall as
Bottom

biggest, richest companies in the world can't do that. So instead of criticising that system I'm confronting it and trying to change it. Theatre should have the freedom to explore like painters do, where you can decide you're in your 'blue period' and throw blue colours on different forms. In the theatre, you just paint one painting at a time. This centre has a freedom – it's just dripping with stuff that we're splashing on all the time and eventually something comes out that you promote. It's a more healthy environment – we're not stuck in a crazy system where the money goes to everything but the stage.

One of the things we have been exploring at La Caserne is working with the internet. We haven't found a shape yet but we're working on it. I believe there's a meeting point between the live and the recorded, that these two are going to merge into one art form. I hope to see this in my lifetime. You can only go so far listening to a record or looking at a film. The audience will want to have a three-dimensional interactive relationship the way they have in theatre. I don't know what it's going to be but I'd really like to be involved. The centre is equipped to do both recorded and live stuff and all of our projects try to combine these two things.

That's what I'm interested in allowing – this thing where you don't care if it's recorded or live, it's the story that gets you and you interact with that. I have my own theory about this. You know, up until the middle of the 19th century painting was the way to chronicle time – to show what the politicians looked like, show the big event, the big battles – that was the job of the painter and nobody could do it better. Then photography came in and says, well, we can do a better, more faithful portrait of this than you can. And quite soon the photography takes over and becomes the chronicler of its time and nobody wants to paint any more, everybody wants to go into photography. For 50 years painting was dead, except that it wasn't dead, it was freed from that burden of being the chronicler – now it can express whatever it wants. Then you start to get Dadaism and Cubism and Impressionism and painting expressing ideas and emotions and concepts that have never been seen before. So I believe that television did not kill drama – television freed drama. Film did not kill theatre – no, theatre is free, and if you don't scare off the artists they'll express ideas that have never been expressed before just like those painters. And that's what really attracts me. That's what I find cool about theatre. It's free, it's not dead. As Frank Zappa would say – Jack is not dead, he just smells funny.

Elsinor Lepage played all the characters in this piece based on **Hamlet**, using excerpts from Shakespeare's work. Believing that his shows are always being created after the opening, Lepage later found great delight in handing the show over to Peter Darling and observing the changes that evolved. When creating **Elsinor** Lepage heard that Robert Wilson was also creating a piece based on **Hamlet**. After an initial stalling, Lepage decided to continue, declaring that there would be two **Hamlets** that year, but they would definitely not be the same.

3

ELSINOR
Created by Robert Lepage
in Montreal, 1995
Nottingham Playhouse,
UK, 1996

1–5 (also pp68–69)
     Robert Lepage

4   5

" . . . if the actors **cannot possess** a piece of theatre it won't **work**"

SIMON McBURNEY

Simon McBurney, described by John Berger as 'the most creative and important theatrical force in Europe', studied at Cambridge and trained at L'École de Mime Jacques Lecoq in Paris. As Artistic Director of Complicite, an award-winning theatre company which he co-founded in 1983, he has devised, directed and performed in over 24 productions that have toured worldwide, including **The Street of Crocodiles**, **The Three Lives of Lucie Cabrol**, and **The Caucasian Chalk Circle**. His production of **The Chairs** played on Broadway and the West End and was nominated for six Tony Awards including Best Director. His most recent work, **Mnemonic**, has won nine awards including a Time Out Live Award for Outstanding Achievement and a Drama Desk Award for Unique Theatrical Experience in New York. The company has worked with many different performer collaborators, but the principles of the work have remained constant – seeking a meeting point between different media, and integrating text, music, image and action to create surprising, disruptive theatre.

Out of a House Walked a Man... brought together an ensemble of actors, musicians and singers for a theatrical concert evoking the world of the writer Daniil Kharms. Kharms' work, his plays, short stories, poems, jokes and fragments of the Russian avant-garde, were swept away by Stalinism in the 1930s.

OUT OF A HOUSE WALKED A MAN...
Devised by Simon McBurney
A co-production with the
Royal National Theatre,
London, UK
Originally performed at the
Lyttelton Theatre, London,
UK, 1994

1 Toby Jones and
   Josef Houben
2 Sophie Grimmer
   and Marcello Magni

1

SIMON McBURNEY: I had a teacher who said to me, 'If an actor has forgotten what it is like to play as a child they should not be an actor.' What the child sees is transformed by imagination. The pattern in a carpet can become a world; a staircase a mountain; and everywhere there are secrets. I grew up without a television. I am sure its absence bent and angled the way I see. What did we do? Read books, sang, and went to bed early. From when we were very small my mother would make theatre with us. So the idea of 'making' your own theatre is something that I grew up with. Every year she would write a pantomime. She would rig up two curtains at the end of a long corridor to make a miniscule playing space. For two weeks we would construct props and costumes, refuse to rehearse when called, play with grease paint in her makeup box and induce a minor yearly nervous breakdown. Cinderella's coach was a transformed tricycle that was painted silver, had a cardboard rococo window attached and trundled a majestic four feet across the stage pulled by ropes running into the kitchen. I do not remember going to the cinema much. My father was fond of renting Laurel and Hardy on 8mm, which I found terrifying. I was convinced that they hurt themselves in their stunts and pratfalls. Playing them backwards at speed was the highlight of the evening. That seemed a lot funnier and more reassuring somehow. The child's imagination is what continues to feed you I think, perhaps because it is fed by an immense curiosity, perhaps because of the wonder. It bends the way you see; it keeps alive an important secret life. Although we *made* theatre, I never envied my mother's role as a director. I don't think it even occurred to me to do so. I was always playing; playing meant imagining; playing involved making; and playing was something that was more fun when you were doing it together with others. That was all. I still think of myself principally as a player, a performer, and an actor; an actor who also directs. Though I tend to think of directing as 'making'. The desire to 'make' I am sure is one reason why I ended up training in Paris.

2

There I saw theatre from everywhere. All theatre seemed to find its way in some form to Paris. At the same time studying with Jacques Lecoq meant that I came in contact with actors, directors, writers, designers and theatre artists from all over the globe. Part of our training required us once a week to devise a ten-minute piece of theatre as a response to the formal part of the week's work. This could be with South Americans and Senegalese one week, Greeks, Italians and Moroccans the next, Australian and Japanese actors the week after. Thus, each week, much of our time would be spent attempting to understand each other and each other's ideas; the difficulty was not so much what we were each saying, (though goodness knows our collective French would have appeared incomprehensible to anyone on the outside) rather it was that even the simplest ideas about theatre were radically different depending on where you were from. Our task became to create a common language. Something that still forms one of the first steps in any production I embark upon. How do you understand each other? How can you find a language for what is often beyond language?

What I learned with Jacques was not only that theatre was a great deal larger and more difficult to define than I had ever conceived in my narrow British upbringing, but that there did appear to be huge areas in common, you could almost say certain universal laws. He opened out the mechanics of theatre for us. But, at the same time, made us understand that theatre is absolutely not mechanical. It is totally unpredictable. And the laws you learn or the rules that you have just created are there to be broken almost immediately.

Based on the stories of Bruno
Schulz; adapted by Simon
McBurney and Mark Wheatley
Royal National Theatre,
London, UK, 1992

1 Hayley Carmichael, Annabel
Arden, Stefan Metz, Joyce
Henderson, Clive Mendus,
Antonio Gil Martinez

SIMON McBURNEY

76

The Street of Crocodiles Based on the
autobiograpical works of Bruno Schulz, *The
Street of Crocodiles* and *Sanatorium under
the sign of the Hour Glass.* Objects and props
took over the rehearsals as the cast explored
Schulz's world. Transformation became a
central theme of the production. A large piece
of cloth was used as the table cloth before
transforming into a beach, the father's
sanatorium bed and finally, yards of material
unfolded to create the sea. During the long
family dinners two actors hung on the wall,
swinging their legs like pendulums.

The movement of theatre is fluid. It is fluid motion. That
becomes random. It is a constantly changing medium.
Turbulent. Chaotic. That is why it is alive. That also is why
Jacques spent so much time with us on looking. Looking at
the movement of the human body. Looking at what happens
in a street. Looking at the great movements of nature, or the
nature of 'the crowd', or how a relationship could reveal itself
in a sequence of looks without words. Or how a word creates
a space, or a space can affect or even produce an emotion.
He would insist we transform what we saw into other shapes.
If the theme of the week was, for example, 'The Street' we
were not always obliged to 'make a drama'. We might be
required to transform what we saw into movement. Not
necessarily in any literal way. Perhaps through dynamic
movement, that is to say in movement that approaches what
would be thought of almost as dance. Even though most of
us were not dancers. Sometimes we would be obliged to
treat what we saw only in terms of 'space'. Or even to talk
about 'space' through the movement of objects such as
sticks, or everyday objects such as chairs and tables.
Much as an architect might do, even though we were not
architects. Or to recreate the tension of what can be seen
with stretched rope or lengths of rubber, like engineers. In
other words, the muscle that he was insisting we exercised
was not only an intellectual, vocal or physical one, it was the
muscle of the imagination. In asking us to work in this way,
we had to become clear. We had to agree upon another way
of seeing, a common vision. Only when you were clear in
what you saw could you be clear about how you chose to
articulate it and then transform it into theatre.

It is the same now in a rehearsal room. First of all we try to
understand what it is that we are trying to understand. As
soon as clarity begins to emerge then the process of putting
it together can be quick. But getting to that point is often
painfully slow. Shostakovitch's dictum resounds in my head:
'Think slowly write quickly.'

Over the time that I have been working with Complicite what
happens in the rehearsal room has changed enormously, yet
certain elements are always present. The constant fooling
around; the immense amount of chaos; pleasure as well as a
kind of turbulent forward momentum. Nothing is off limits
apart from not turning up. It is often extremely unstructured,

2

THE THREE LIVES OF LUCIE CABROL
Based on a story by John
Berger; adapted by Simon
McBurney and Mark Wheatley
First performed at The
Dancehouse, Manchester,
UK, 1994

2 Lilo Baur and Simon McBurney
3 Simon McBurney and Lilo Baur

3

The Three Lives of Lucie Cabrol Here again
McBurney used the transformation of objects
to resolve a staging challenge, in this case
the protagonists making love in a barn: 'we
suddenly seized the planks we were holding
to represent the barn they were in, and
started to fling them around the rehearsal
room. The wall came apart and planks
flew across the stage and we found the
dynamic of love-making transposed into the
explosion of the space and the movement
of the objects.'

though paradoxically quite disciplined. The room is crammed full of stuff; on the walls pictures, text, photographs, videos, objects, clothes and paper everywhere… But this is by no means a consistent picture. Often we reach a moment when there must be nothing in the room at all. It has to be bare, empty and uncluttered. So when rehearsing a piece I do not have a method, no single approach. Ultimately the material dictates each rehearsal.

For example, an early piece, **A Minute Too Late**, was about death, the experience of death. Something I had just gone through with my father. Perhaps it merited some research quietly in a remote room. But in fact the show was to grow out of four days' improvisation that we did in front of art students at the Royal College of Art. We found ourselves making people roar with laughter from day one. The weight of the subject did not create expected conditions. We hardly thought about what we were talking about. The subject simply talked through what we did. We had the strange sensation that the show wrote itself. What is certain is that it sprang from the frenzied non-stop action of those few days.

In contrast, when making **The Chairs** with Richard Briers and Geraldine MacEwan, we sat. Not making people laugh. Sitting. Even though it is in essence a totally ridiculous cabaret-esque action-dominated farce. There appeared to nothing amusing about it at all. For weeks we were terrified that the piece would not work, would not be in the least bit funny. So we had to approach it as if in total seriousness, looking to make what was apparently meaningless as clear as an instruction manual to a lawnmower. That is what the material needed, that kind of textual attention. Out of the absurd mire of Ionesco's language we had to painstakingly unearth a sober sense before we could then let ourselves loose on the ridiculous, and transform it once more. We had to find a common language with Ionesco, which could be transformed into theatre.

The Street of Crocodiles was based on the short stories of Bruno Schulz. Our starting point here was simply to read to each other. Then we attempted to experience and re-create the stories in a myriad forms and guises. Beginning by telling and retelling the stories. In abbreviated forms; or as fireside tales – as evocations of 'The World of Bruno' and visions without words at all, as dreams and nightmares. But in this rehearsal the objects began to dominate. They took over the room, filling pockets and the insides of the actors' hats, or

80

under their tables. Umbrellas, books sprouting feathers, boots, glasses and cutlery. In retrospect I realised that Schulz's vision, which evokes the transforming power of the child's eye, necessarily meant that objects and their transmogrification would be central to the process. But when we were in it, they seemed to take over the whole process without permission, beyond our control. I remember struggling with the attempt to bring the text to the fore with my co-adaptor Mark Wheatley. There were evenings of despair at the apparently unequal nature of the struggle. It was the material that pushed us there, the unruly unrepentant skew of Schulz's imagination which was both impetus and goal, and which we were, quite rightly, to be governed by.

Transformation was one of the subject matters of **The Street of Crocodiles**. But transformation, or the transforming nature of theatre is something that is essential. To be able to evoke another world through the simplest of means is not only marvellous, but, I think, part of the meaning of theatre. Why? In **Mnemonic** we had to represent a 5000-year-old corpse that emerges brown and wrinkled out of a glacier in 1992. It became clear to us that any literal representation would be more than faintly ludicrous. The words alone that described his appearance were stronger than any banal prop. But something had to stand in for his presence. So we used a chair. But the chair was more evocative if broken. So we used a broken chair. But then we felt it would be marvellous if

it could move in some way. And so it was transformed by a puppet maker into a 'chair/man'. A chair that also evoked the space and limbs of the iceman when operated like a Bunraku puppet (as in the traditional Japanese puppet theatre). It is marvellous when a chair becomes a human being. That is clear. People marvel. Literally. I, too, am astonished, that for the audience the five people operating the chair, making it 'walk' and 'fall', should somehow disappear so that all we see is the man. But what is more marvellous is what it reveals. That theatre does not exist up there, up here on the stage. That is not the space of theatre. The space of theatre is in the minds of the audience. It is what separates this art form from all others. Not the fact that we imagine something to be there when it is not, nor the fact that we suspend our disbelief, but the fact that we do it together… in the same moment.

We are all alone. We all spend much of our lives trying to reach out to others with, at the same time, a profound sense of our own solitude. Yet in the theatre, at moments of genuine transformation, as we all 'see' the same thing at the same moment, we touch the solitary imaginations of our neighbours and so for a brief moment we too are transformed, by the sense and realisation that we are not alone. We are not mere individuals but part of a community. Perhaps, somewhere within us, we might even recognise that this is an event that had always been part of the human condition. And so we sense that we are not only part of a community, but also part of a continuity.

1

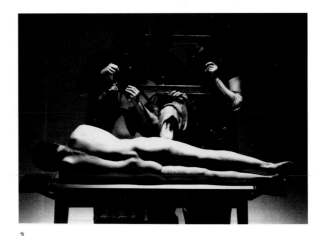

2

3

Mnemonic Here, McBurney used the theatre to bring together the 'shards' of stories that bombard us every day, fragmented by television, radio, print and the internet. 'I wanted to give people a sense of something having disappeared into the past, so I spoke into a microphone and turned away. At that point there was an invisible cut with a pre-recorded piece of conversation. So what people thought was live immediately disappeared into the past as the character sat there listening to what had just been said. That's a way of using technology but keeping it theatrical.'

MNEMONIC
Conceived by Simon
McBurney; devised by
the company
A co-production with the
Salzburg Festival, Austria
Originally performed at the
Lawrence Batley Theatre,
Huddersfield, 1999

(also pp78–79)

4

People often ask where we begin. We always begin with a text. But that text can take many forms. Perhaps, for example, it was something to do with community and continuity that started **Mnemonic**. I had wanted to make a piece about memory for many years. At the source, we merely investigated our own memories and how they functioned. How much do you remember? How far back does your memory go? To your childhood? Beyond into your parent's childhood? If memory is not possible without consciousness, and our conscious selves are created by our backgrounds and where we come from, how does what we remember tell us who we are. And if we forget where we come from, what continuity we are part of? Does that mean we forget who we are?

So the root of the piece in this instance was our own experience. It was about what we remembered, about where we came from. That was our text. But it became more complicated. I had also been fascinated with the discovery of the 5000-year-old Neolithic corpse in the Austrian Alps,

written up by the archaeologist Konrad Spindler as 'The Man in the Ice'. And Rebecca West's journey to Yugoslavia in the 1930s. And Hans Magnus Enzensberger's musings on civil war at the end of the 20th century. And without knowing exactly how we would do it we began to connect these and many other texts together… until the piece emerged.

When I say the text can be many things – I mean it can equally well be a visual text, a text of action, a musical one, as well as the more conventional one involving plot and characters. 'Theatre,' says Aristotle, 'is an act and an action.' Action is also a text. As is the space, the light, music, the sound of footsteps, silence and immobility. All should be as articulate and evocative as each other.

I have often heard people say that as a company we are fascinated by action and image. But that is only because what people *do* must be as clear as what they *say*. I do not mean that what they do must copy language. But just as poetry is central in much of the theatrical canon, so what people *do* can also be couched in its own poetic transformation. In **The Three Lives of Lucie Cabrol** we encountered the problem of the representation of the protagonists, Jean and Lucie, making love in a barn. All our solutions were either embarrassing or clichéd, until, under the pressure of the final weeks, we suddenly seized the planks we were holding to represent the barn they were in, and started to fling them around the rehearsal room. The wall came apart and planks flew across the stage and we found the dynamic of love-making transposed into the explosion of the space and the movement of the objects.

These are examples plucked at random from years of graft. Most of the time such moments of revelation or discovery are rare. And there are more weeks of despair than seconds of elation. In such moments I long to be told what to do. Or to disappear down the corridor and play with the curtains or dive into the makeup box, and let someone else decide for me. A piece of theatre is, ultimately, in the hands of those who are performing it. The actors. It is they, not the director, who must have the whole piece in their every gesture, hearing the meaning in each word. And to do that I think, as an actor, you have to feel that you possess the piece. And to possess the piece you have to be part of its creation. Involved intimately in the process of its making.

I had the fortune to act with Paul Eddington on his last job. He wrinkled his nose when I told him that after acting in this piece I would be directing. 'What do you want from a director then?' I asked.
'I only require one thing.'
'What is that?'
'Confidence.'

Confidence. Confidence with which to make us believe that we see a world in a pattern on a carpet; or a staircase as a mountain; and secrets everywhere.

Copyright Simon McBurney July 2002

2

83

THE CHAIRS
By Eugene Ionesco
A co-production with the
Royal Court Theatre
Originally performed at the
Bath Theatre Royal, 1997

1–2 Geraldine MacEwan and
Richard Briers in rehearsal

The Chairs McBurney thoroughly enjoyed working with Geraldine MacEwan and Richard Briers; 'I had to work with them on ideas of physical articulation; if it became clear in the text that such and such was required then of course they'd lie on the floor and do different exercises. They'd play games and so on, in order to release the games that are played between the characters. Geraldine loved everything I threw at her. I'd ask her to do this or that, or improvise – she didn't care, she roared with laughter!'

1

The Visit McBurney
performed in this piece
which he co-directed with
Annabel Arden. The
production evolved out of
comic improvision and a
fixation with the transfomation
of objects.

2

THE VISIT
By Friedrich Durrenmatt;
adapted by Maurice Valency
Co-directed with Annabel
Arden
Originally performed at the
Almeida Theatre, London,
UK, 1991

1   Simon McBurney
2   Kathryn Hunter

"theatre
should be given back
to the actors"

YUKIO NINAGAWA

Yukio Ninagawa established himself as a director of some merit in 1969 with a Japanese 'agitational company', the Contemporary People's Theatre, with whom he worked for four years. In 1973 he moved over to the commercial theatre, joining forces with the producer Tadao Nakane of the Toho Group and went on to direct **Oedipus**,1976, **Macbeth**, 1980, and **Medea**, 1983, which was slated by the Japanese critics and led to a loss of confidence. Fortunately, Nakane persuaded him to take the production abroad to Athens, where it received great critical acclaim, and was subsequently invited to tour internationally. He has since gone on to produce many productions both of Western classics and contemporary Japanese works, including **Tango at the End of Winter** with a British company where he formed a close working relationship with the producer Thelma Holt. Ninagawa won the Grand Prize at The Arts Festival in Japan for his production of Matsuyo Akimoto's **Cikamatu Shinju-Monogatari** (Suicide for Love). Other awards include the Arts Encouragement Prize by the Japanese Minister of Education, 1987, and an honorary doctorate from the University of Edinburgh in 1991.

YUKIO NINAGAWA: As a child I was taken to the theatre – kabuki, ballet, opera – by my mother. During and after the war, mothers were starving for some good culture from the West – it was like hunting for food. My mother would say, 'don't worry about school' and pick me up from elementary school and take me out. So I became very familiar with culture. In Japan it is customary for the middle classes to support poor artists, so as a child, I saw the works of many young painters in my house. My father was a tailor and he displayed painters' works in his shop, like a gallery, and customers would come and buy them. My family was very proud of this, and, as I wasn't doing well at school, I thought I'd be a painter myself. I took an entrance exam to a famous art school but failed. It was at this point that I thought, OK, how about becoming an actor?

So, when I was 19, I discovered a small avant-garde theatre, which had a training programme. I auditioned, got in and studied Stanislavski and Brecht. I was an actor for 11 years but I had no talent and didn't enjoy it – I always felt too self-conscious. In Japan, at that time, there were many new theatre practitioners all wanting to create a new Japanese theatre, different to that in Europe. I wanted to be a part of this, so I decided to become a director. When I told the theatre company they said, 'you're not a good actor, so you won't be a good director either,' but I left, took some young actors who respected me and together we formed the Contemporary People's Theatre.

In 1969, in a Tokyo district called Shinju-ku there was a cinema that performed late-night avant-garde theatre. This was where I made my debut as a director with Kunio Shimizu's **Sincere Frivolity**. The place was tiny, the stage just 2 metres deep and the auditorium about 4.3 metres. The actors were a combination of professionals, students and people you just picked up off the streets. It was also a period of student riots and one night the riot police clashed with students during the play. The audience was amazed when riot police came in, and the students were so excited that they demonstrated and marched through the audience, between the seats. Very exciting, thrilling theatre. I stayed with the company until 1973 when I was asked to direct **Romeo and Juliet** for the commercial theatre. My company felt I was betraying them. They believed that underground theatre should remain underground but I had felt it was time to go for a while. There should have been the freedom to go

MEDEA
By Euripides
Worldwide, 1983 to present

1–2 Traditional all-male cast
with Tokusaburo Arashi as
Medea
3 Tokusaburo Arashi

3

89

Medea Ninagawa used the original Japanese theatrical style of an all-male cast for this performance of **Medea**. Performed in Ancient Greek the production combined Western style with the Japanese theatrical techniques of Kabuki and Bunraku. Influences for the costume design came from the bright orange tunics of ancient-Greek red-figure vases. Medea changed into red half way through the play and eventually disrobed to allow the audience to see the male actor's body (3).

back and forth, because that's the way to make changes in theatre and truly develop.

Commercial theatre life was very different. At first I didn't sit in the chair made for the director – I put a newspaper on the floor and squatted there! I was used to making coffee, even cleaning the rehearsal room myself. I found the actors very lazy – they didn't even learn their lines. I would say, 'I won't start rehearsing until you've learnt your lines.' When we started to block they were reluctant to get up to rehearse and they would even sometimes be wearing slippers. In Japan we take off our shoes to go into a house and wear slippers inside but I got really angry when they were coming in as Romeo and Juliet wearing slippers! Then they were reluctant to project fully from the heart because they did not want to damage their voices. 'Speak up,' I would tell them. I would throw ashtrays – sometimes chairs – at those who didn't! It was a really serious battle changing the custom of those actors.

You see, in those days I had to be forceful and even violent but now I want actors to work in an environment where they extend their imaginations and creativity, and have no fear. I like to make actors feel they can do anything. On the first day of rehearsals we read the text. I tell the actors how I interpret the play and how I wish to present it and then we have a discussion. The next day we start to rehearse on an actual-size set which has been mocked up in the rehearsal room. I always say to the actors, 'It's there, right in front of you. I give you the framework so now please go and act in the way you interpret the text – read the text in your body.' Actors should be motivated by the words *and* body; they're not separate things. When I work with English actors they are often puzzled. 'How should I move?' they ask. 'You think,' I tell them. 'I won't give you instructions.'

Set and costume designers are with me in rehearsals every day ready to make changes as needed and the stage crew are also there to rehearse scene changes as we go. Of course, we do conceptual work during rehearsals but it is always backed up with practical, tangible, material things like actors, props and set.

I use young staff, much younger than me, people who love developing and growing. For a long time I have been using only two creative teams, Horio and Nakagoshi, both different

HINOTORI
Based on a story by
Osamu Tezuka
Saitama Super Arena, Japan
Designed by Yukio Horio

1–3 Sketches by Yukio Horio
4–5 The spectacle in Saitama

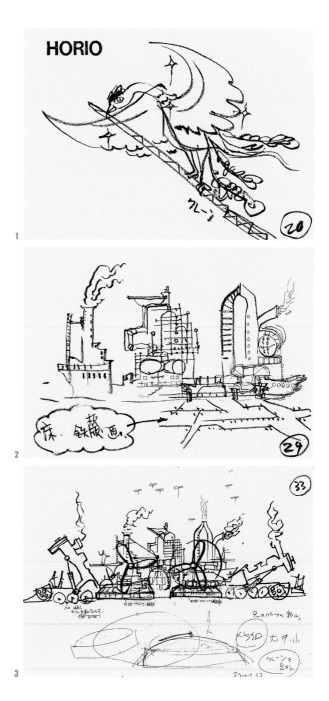

1

2

3

4

Hinotori This musical spectacle was performed in the enormous 37,000-seater stadium in Saitama, newly opened in 2000. Based on an original story by the famous Manga cartoonist Osama Tezuka, the themes explored mankind's odyssy: life, death, rebirth and love. The designer, Yukio Horio, a frequent collaborator with Ninagawa, filled the stage with a dramatic industrial-themed set, which sought to encompass a timeline that leapt between Genesis, the present and the future and which evoked the eerie atmosphere of Ridley Scott's *Bladerunner*. Cranes were used to move parts of the set between scenes.

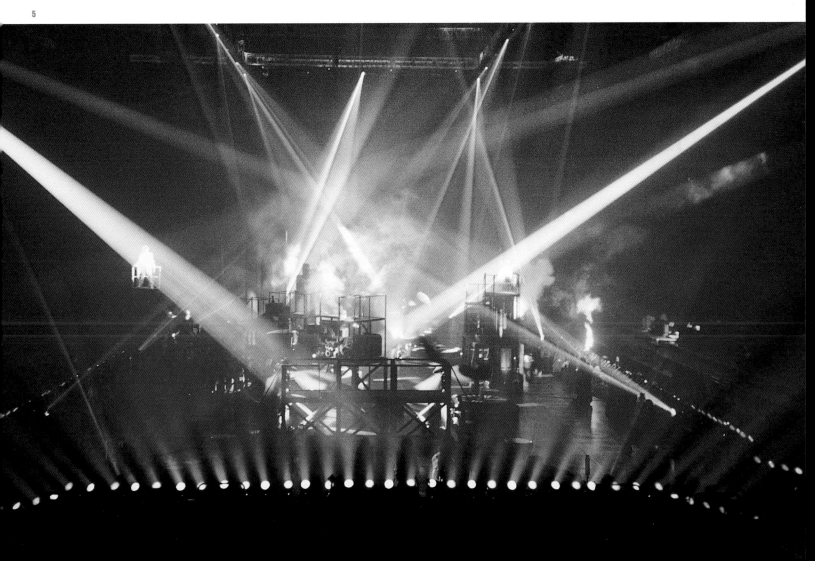

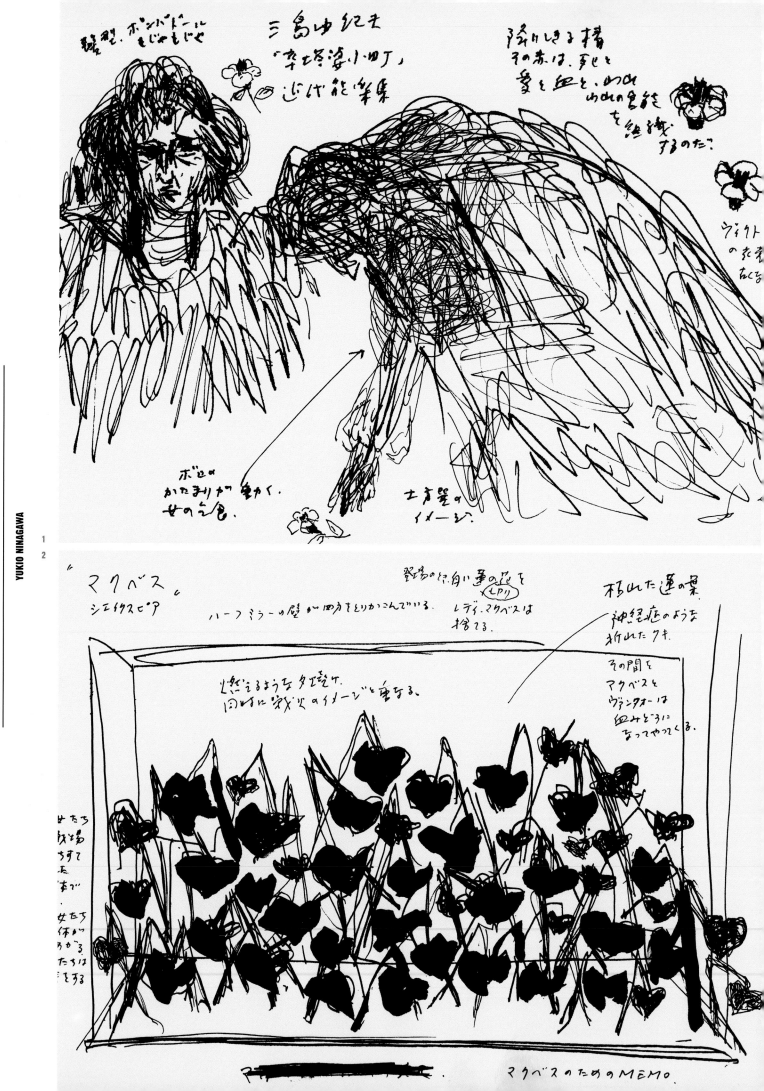

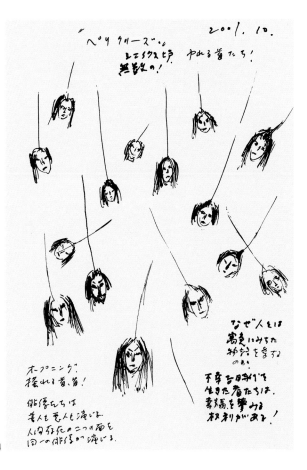

1 SOTOBA KOMACHI
By Yukio Mishima

This sketch by Ninagawa for the modern Noh play **Sotoba Komachi** is accompanied by notes on the themes and ideas explored in the early stages of the production. The notes translate: 'Hair style – pompadour, ragged, fluffy; the camelia flowers are tumbling, the red representing death, love, blood and the mountain's sexuality; the costume is old Victorian style; the bank of rubbish is moving, revealing a woman beggar; image of Hijikata Hajime.'

2 MACBETH
By William Shakespeare
Shiga Hokaido, Japan, 1996

Here Ninagawa explores the themes of death and deception. His notes read: 'The wall, made of half mirrors, surrounds all sides of the stage; Lady Macbeth cuts the white lotus flowers as she enters; dead leaves of lotus flowers; Macbeth and Banquo walk through these flowers with the bloody body; intense sunset like fire that reminds you of an image of fire in war; the witches are actually dead bodies discarded at the battle field; the dead bodies of women in the village stand up and make prophecies.'

3 YOTUYAKAIDAN
Traditional Japanese story
Theatre Cocoon, Tokyo, 2001

For this ghost story Ninagawa used a Western staging device to tell a traditional Japanese story. A summary of his notes reads: 'A rearrangement of the classics; the first Japanese play with this structure; Japanese house with a wall of mirrors; Oiwa's face is reflected in the mirrors; the figure of the murderer Izaemon; Naosuke who raped his little sister; the image of Osode who fell into Hell; see through the structure; Kabuki house in Edo era; people make the stage rotate under the floor.'

4 PERICLES
By William Shakespeare
Sai No Kuni Saitama Art Theatre, Saitama, and Royal National Theatre, London, 2003

Ningawa explored another dramatic device for the opener of this Shakespeare play: 'Innumerable swinging heads; the actors play both a good one and a bad one, the two aspects of human existence; why do people love a story so full of morality?; those living in an unhappy era have the right to dream of a better life.'

generations. Horio, the older one, completely fills the stage from one corner to the other. I never accept his first ideas but after discussion they always get better and better. With Nakagoshi, the younger one, I discuss the work a lot so it doesn't take a wrong direction, but I know it's always going to have some sense of the younger generation about it. I have only very simple discussions with the lighting designer. I'll say, 'I don't want too many colours,' or 'let's use a lot of colour this time.' Sometimes they hang lights in the rehearsal room to try things out. It all comes together in the dress rehearsal but that takes a long time. When the lighting was completed on a production of **King Lear**, prior to the one at the Barbican, I realised there was no sense of 'theatre discovery'. So I asked all the staff to gather round and said, 'you are just copying your own work – let's change the set, the lighting, everything.' For three nights we didn't sleep and we made it again, the whole composition. The result was really good.

There are no plays like Shakespeare's in Japan. There is no other playwright who makes the actors the core of the drama, so we have no dramaturgy in the European sense. In the early years I tried to change the commercial sector by putting on Shakespeare, Greek tragedy, and Brecht – playwrights that the commercial theatre would not normally take up. But all the critics hated it. They would say, 'this is nothing like Shakespeare done in England or Greek tragedy done in Greece.' My desire was to convey Shakespeare or Greek plays to the Japanese audience not as academic works, something we had to learn, but as theatre.

One of my favourite pieces of work is **A Midsummer Night's Dream**. In the seventies I saw a production directed by Peter Brook, with its white box and swings, and thought, one day I'm going to make a completely different 'dream sequence'. I made it in 1990 and set it in a rock garden, inspired by the Duonji Temple garden in Kyoto. In Japan the rock garden represents our spirit, the cosmos, so in Peter Brook's 'dream' the fairies came from the top but in mine they came from the ground. I also had sand coming down from the sky like thread, representing time. There was a mixture of old and new, to give Shakespeare both a classical and a modern feel. The actors wore a combination of European and Japanese costume, an outer garment and a very shabby,

1

KING LEAR
By William Shakespeare
Royal Shakespeare Company,
Stratford-upon-Avon,
UK, 1999
Designed by Yukio Horio

1 The set for Act 1
2 Sketch by designer Yukio
  Horio for Act 4
3 Act 4, Sc 2, Nigel
  Hawthorne as King Lear
  and Hiroyuki Sanada as
  the fool

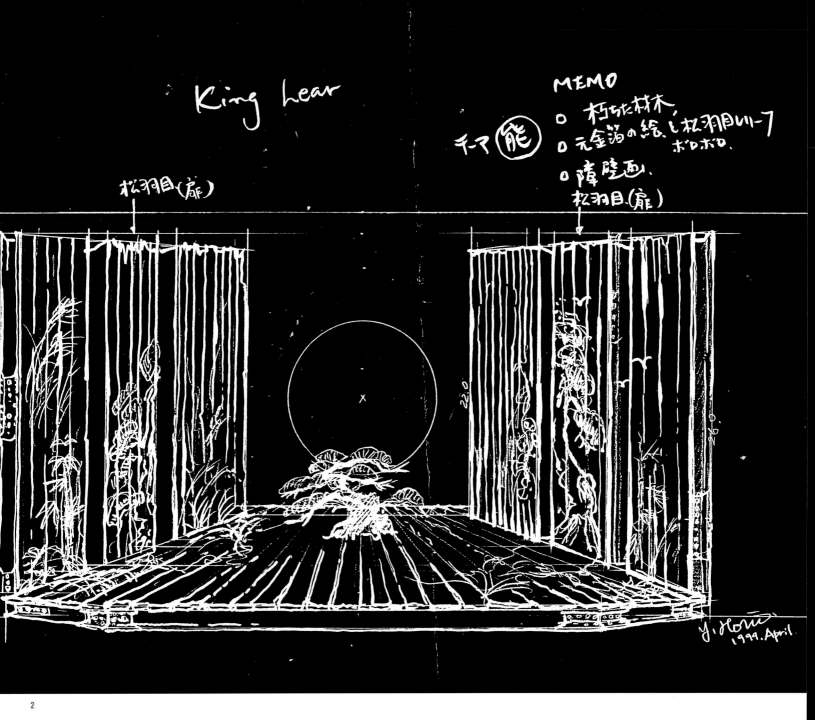

King Lear

松羽目（扉）

MEMO
○ 朽ちた材木、
○ 元金箔の絵 と 松羽目いー-7
ボロボロ。
○ 障壁画。
松羽目（扉）

テーマ 能

x

2.0

Y.Horio
1999.April

King Lear Working on the RSC's production of **King Lear** highlighted the differences between the Japanese and English actors for Ninagawa: 'English actors don't move unless there's a reason; the Japanese actors move and then add the reason later. There's always something concrete, tangible, between me and English actors, but in Japan good actors move very freely.' However, Ninagawa found his experience working with English actors very enjoyable. Part of the rehearsal period was spent in Japan so he could give them a better understanding of the Japanese methods of working.

3

1

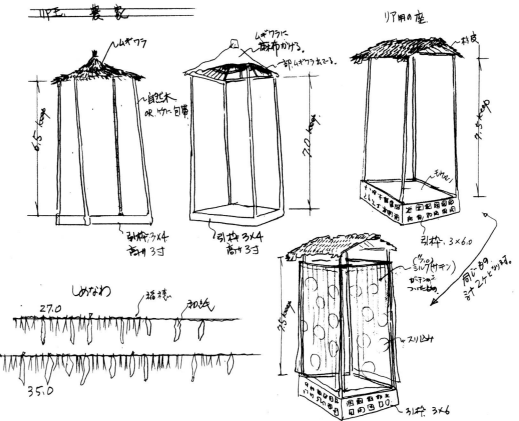

2

toned-down kabuki costume and they rode on bikes and scooters. It was very working-class and realistic, yet, at the same time, very aristocratic. We put it on at the Mermaid Theatre in London and the audience loved it.

I often use European methods of realism when I do naturalistic plays, but, when I want to make a play stylised I go for kabuki or Noh theatre. For instance, in my production of **Sotoba Komachi** by Mishima, I changed space and time from one moment to another using a back curtain that drops. We call it the kabuki curtain for the sake of the English crew. It's a very traditional kabuki method. Also, in my production of **Medea** the chorus is covered in a big cloth so you can't actually see the body shapes. The actors keep their knees bent as they walk so that they appear to slide across the floor. They can't move up and down, they can only move on one level. Traditional Japanese theatre is very cruel to the bodies; there's always tension somewhere. I think the reason is that we used to do more tragedies and you maintain the tragic element by concentrating tension in the centre of your body.

You see, in most traditional Japanese theatre it is a pleasure to cry because you are crying at someone else's misfortune – that's how you forget about your own. But these days a lot of theatre is about laughing, like cheap television comedy. I get irritated with the state of Japanese theatre because it is so influenced by television and there's so much electronic media now. If you get too carried away with the lighting and electronic development, you forget about the actors. At the moment I feel that theatre should be given back to the actors, so my sets are getting simpler and I am putting more demands on the actors. They are happening right there in front of you. That is what theatre is about.

KING LEAR
By William Shakespeare
Royal Shakespeare Company,
Stratford-upon-Avon,
UK, 1999
Designed by Yukio Horio

1 Nigel Hawthorne
2 Sketch of the shelters
  by Yukio Horio
3 Nigel Hawthorne and
  Hiroyuki Sanada

3

"I want to **go on** looking at **anything** and everything without a signature."

TREVOR NUNN

Trevor Nunn studied English at Cambridge University. On leaving in 1962 he won an ABC Scholarship as a director trainee at Belgrade Theatre, Coventry. In 1964 he went straight to the Royal Shakespeare Company and became associate director the following year, becoming the youngest ever Artistic Director of the RSC in 1968. He stayed in that post until 1986. Nunn achieved international fame alongside his collaborator John Caird with the eight-hour drama **Nicholas Nickleby** and the musical **Les Misérables** which has been seen all over the world. He has directed the world premières of four Andrew Lloyd Webber musicals: **Cats**, **Starlight Express**, **Aspects of Love** and **Sunset Boulevard**. In 1997 Nunn was appointed Artistic Director of the Royal National Theatre where he created a repertory company producing such classics as **Summerfolk**, **The Merchant of Venice** and **Troilus and Cressida**. In 2002 he relinquished his post at the RNT to concentrate on a freelance career.

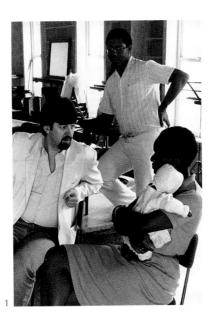

PORGY AND BESS
Music by George Gershwin
Glyndeborne Festival Opera,
UK, 1986

1 Trevor Nunn in rehearsal
   with Cynthia Haymon
   (Bess)

TREVOR NUNN: I have never had any sympathy for the directional approach that sets out to create unease or fear in the belief that thereby extraordinary things can be achieved. Instead, it's a conscious aim of mine to create an inclusive, productive and above all happy atmosphere in the rehearsal room. I believe the rehearsal process must be collaborative and that everybody present has the right to a voice.

Complex textual work like, say, work on a mature Shakespeare tragedy, benefits from all the actors involved being available for and open to every kind of insight and that means there must be a genuine equality in the rehearsal room, owing nothing to hierarchy or deference. Of course, certain roles bear greater responsibility than others and the thoughts and instincts of those actors will be central, but not exclusively so.

Direction is more concerned with analysis than anything else, analysis supported by preparation, including the vastly important preparatory period of casting. Once the material has been the subject of the directional x-ray, then choices from amongst the density of actor-generated responses can be made to identify and support the structure of the play. Decision making in rehearsal must not be, nor appear to be, whimsical or temperamental, but rather maintain a balance between instinctive engagement and detailed intellectual analysis.

I remember Peter Hall describing the director's relationship to the work as 'benevolent dictatorship' and I recognise that conclusion. As in a democracy, there is in the preparation of a play a shared requirement for nurturing things to happen through agreement. Ultimately though, the democracy of majority opinion has to be replaced by the director's shaping and interpretative decisions. It will always be preferable if the necessary taking of the reins is more or less unnoticeable, particularly in the case of music theatre, wherein so many disciplines vie for dominance.

In truth, most forms of theatre (in my experience) require design decisions ahead of rehearsals because of time constraints on workshops, and therefore many elements of a production are a *fait accompli* for the actors. It is a great luxury, frightening because of its rarity, to begin with a group of actors, a text and everything else, as it were, a blank sheet. Most memorably, I enjoyed this luxury with the production of the epic stage version of **Nicholas Nickleby**. The origin of the production was prosaic, and lay in the necessity for me to find only one show to satisfy the needs of a fifty-strong company, because the money had run out to do the four or five new shows which were necessary to honour my contractual obligations. A play providing genuine acting challenges for fifty people has never been written, but it occurred to me at the moment of crisis that the answer might be in something I had thought of doing several years before, adapting the teeming human multiplicity of a Dickens novel to the stage.

We started with no script, and therefore no design, and indeed no casting. The moment when almost the entire resident acting company arrived at the first rehearsal (though they had no contractual obligation to do so) was the most moving and gratifying of my 18 years of running the RSC.

My colleague John Caird and I began with copies of Dickens' *Nicholas Nickleby* and the knowledge that we had a few

Macbeth was one of Nunn's greatest sucesses when he was directing for the Royal Shakespeare Company. Ian McKellen was voted Actor of the Year for his role of Macbeth. The production has gone down in history as one of the best adaptations of this play.

MACBETH
By William Shakespeare
Royal Shakespeare Company,
Stratford-upon-Avon, UK,
1976

2 Ian McKellen as Macbeth
3 Ian McKellen and Judi
   Dench as Lady Macbeth

NICHOLAS NICKLEBY
By Trevor Nunn and
John Caird
Royal Shakespeare Company,
Stratford-upon-Avon, and
Aldwych Theatre, London, UK

4 Graham Crowden and
   Roger Rees (pp102–103)

4

months to find with the actors a theatre language for this richly comedic sprawling tentacular material. We challenged ourselves to confront particularly difficult or seemingly impossible sequences in the novel, and through games and improvisation often of an almost abstract quality, we began to make choices. We appointed David Edgar to be our writer in rehearsal, and for many weeks he observed and notated our increasingly confident and recognisable improvisational scenes. Only when David's 'play' had taken shape did we address with John Napier the issue of design, knowing in advance our extreme budgetary limitations. It was indeed exhilarating to be making a work of theatre in the right order, and in a way that, despite our crisis and desperation, most theatre organisations in the world would be unable to provide for. The eventual triumph of the project changed the image of the RSC, and ironically pointed the company towards a much more secure financial future.

Again, when I directed **Not About Nightingales**, an early never-performed play by the young Tennessee Williams, astonishingly brought to light by the intrepid detective work of Vanessa Redgrave, there was no production design or resolved method of presenting its very demanding scenes when rehearsals began. Our work was improvisational, exploring the rituals and extremities of prison life to which the text gave at times only barely coherent expression. Eventually there was enough physical evidence from the rehearsal room enquiry to allow the designer, Richard Hoover, to give it form – which eventually for the audience became a tangibly oppressive and brutalised experience.

It has been a long time now since I haven't embarked on some improvisational work as a way in to more formal and textual rehearsal. Even in my recent National Theatre production of Vanbrugh's **The Relapse**, there was an element of improvisation in the creation of a self-confident troupe of 17th-century players, who could mingle with the arriving audience, communicating scandal, intrigue and louche small talk in highly wrought but spontaneous language.

Continuity, building up a vocabulary and method with largely the same group of actors after a number of productions, leads to work of experiment and improvisation of a sophisticated kind; everybody involved can readily acknowledge that the work is picking up where they left off. But in the English theatre, even at a highly subsidised organisation like the RNT, it is most often the case that the director is starting each production with an ad hoc group of actors, a diverse and nervous group who, perforce, must be turned quickly into a coherent company. I feel guilty sometimes, at putting unsuspecting actors through the hoops of company building games, but in every case I can think of, the process quickly pays off; breakthroughs of trust and courage occur amidst an atmosphere of mutual respect and good humour.

As recently as the RNT production of **South Pacific** – which could be approached as a standard Broadway musical, requiring standard techniques – I brought the company together through improvisation enquiring into the conditions on a small Pacific island in 1943. For several days we established the sensations of acclimatising to temperatures in excess of 100 degrees, of segregation between men and women, the daily military rituals, the disciplines of the latrines and washing areas, the limited social calendar and, of course, the traditions and practices of island life. Climactically, each actor was able to improvise 24 hours in the life of his or her character before they had even sung a note or danced a step.

A disparate group assembled from different countries of origin and different artistic backgrounds demonstrated astonishing integrity and commitment through this work and cohered into a unit more in the skin of their characters than they had thought possible in such a brief period of time. Thereafter, staging, including choreographic staging, derived from strong improvisational input, with the actors wanting to bring the scenes alive themselves, without waiting for instruction.

But one kind of work is never a substitute for another. There is no substitute when working on a Shakespeare play for detailed scholastically responsible textual investigation. Every possibility of meaning, in nuance, resonance, tone, echo, image cluster; every value of verse structure, of prose creating dynamics in contrast to the iambic line, must be

2

SOUTH PACIFIC
By Rodgers & Hammerstein
Royal National Theatre,
London, UK, 2001

1 'Wash that Man' with
   Lauren Kennedy
2 Edward Baker-Duly and
   Elaine Tan

expounded and shared. The actors must be conversant with the implicit rules of heightened Elizabethan language if they are eventually to break them, with effect and intention. A mighty and seemingly indestructible text can fall apart at the smallest invitation.

I enjoy spending time, a long time, sitting with actors around a table exclusively on textual study. Recently on **The Merchant of Venice** at the RNT I spent ten days at this work, setting free every hidden possibility of meaning we could discern, and encouraging in the process a wealth of anecdotal insight from everybody in the company.

I really don't like to categorise myself as somebody with a particular or identifiable style, or from whom one particular

CATS
Based on *Old Possums Book of Practical Cats* by T. S. Eliot
Music composed by Andrew Lloyd Webber; designed by John Napier
Winter Garden, London, UK, 1982 to present

1

2

kind of work is expected. I don't like the idea of having a trademark or even a signature. Directors must, for the most part, serve writers, and I fear we fail to serve the writer when we promote, above all things, the directorial signature; the highly recognisable directorial stamp regardless of whether or not it is consistent with the material. But this is not to say that I frown on interpretation. I think it is vital that a production has an explicit take on the material, and I can hardly claim otherwise. I have done Shakespeare plays in many and various emphatic interpretative guises, including productions in modern dress, as with **Timon of Athens** or **The Comedy of Errors**, or futuristically as with **The Winter's Tale** or with a kind of fictional modernity as with **Macbeth** or **Hamlet**. I believe that revitalising the familiar play can come about through reinterpretation and indeed through relocation into found or intimate spaces. But what governs these choices must be thematic, and analytically sound. For example, a passionate production of The Tempest as a tirade against colonialism will always come unstuck, because most of the play either isn't about that, or it is actively in conflict with that interpretative notion.

There are many plays I still yearn to do, **The Tempest** being prime among them, or do again, including **Hamlet**, which I think of as unfinished business. My appetite for demanding new plays has increased. I look forward to being involved in a new musical work, and to once again relinquishing the cares of state to become an artist subject not to the needs of the organisation but only to my imagination. But whatever I do, I hope it will be without a signature.

Cats T. S. Eliot's short book about cats was an unlikely subject for a musical, but with the music of Andrew Lloyd Webber and the design of John Napier, Nunn's production became one of the biggest musical successes ever known. Nunn was also the lyricist for the show's best-known song 'Memory' which was left out of the original book because Eliot thought Grizabella too sad a character. The show has lasted twenty years and looks set to remain a permanent feature of London's West End.

"**Theatre** is about offering **time,** closing the **door,** blocking **the daylight out,** and **concentrating** for three or four hours, in **one situation."**

PETER STEIN

Peter Stein was born in Berlin in 1937. After studying at the University of Munich he assisted Hans Schweikart and Fritz Kortner at the Munich Kammerspiele before staging his debut production, the German première of **Saved** by Edward Bond. He participated in the foundation of the Berliner Schaubuhne where he formed a core company of actors and experimented with applying concepts of a collective structure to the running of a theatre and the creative process, encouraging true collaboration with everyone involved. His high level of artistic expression was once referred to as one of the 'greatest innovations since Brecht'. Between 1991 and 1997 he was the director of the theatre department at the Salzburg Festival in Austria. Recent work includes **Hamlet** (Moscow), 1998, and the 21-hour-long production of **Faust** (Hanover, Berlin, Vienna) at the internationally acclaimed 2000 Hanover Exposition.

PETER STEIN: My political beliefs and my artistic beliefs are linked but they are not the same. Because theatre is about questioning, about contrast, about making yourself and other people absolutely certain about what you are thinking and believing; because theatre is about the truth of the existence of mankind and not about different political convictions. This is the big problem of an interpretation so unilateral of what is 'left' and what is art, and I suffered all my career over this stupidity. It meant a lot, because I am also myself rather stupid and made a lot of faults in this direction. As I grew older I became cautious in the conclusions, but the basic convictions are the same; I never moved away from them. And why should I? Because I think my political convictions are based on humanism, so I don't see how they can change. The condition of mankind in this world will never change; it will have different aspects, but the basic situation is exactly the same. We are between birth and death and nothing else. The Greek tragedy speaks exactly about this tragic situation, and the theatre is founded to tell stories about this basic problem.

I started to do theatre because I didn't want to work alone, which meant that, for me, doing theatre was a social process. I need the collaboration and the opinions of other people. And so the basis of my work is to find and execute projects in a way that will involve participants in all the artistic decisions. My theatre that I had for 15 years was organised collectively and all the artistic decisions were done together, with the possibility also to vote against me, the organiser and the leader. When I left this theatre and worked just creating one show it became clear that the decisions about the technical things like space, scenography and costumes are taken before rehearsals because time is needed to construct them.

I always designed my own stage and the set designer was an executor of my decisions of how the space should be organised; because I am convinced that every show needs its own space. Therefore, I always tried to stay in places where I could be totally mobile and place the audience in any situation. I constructed theatres, quite a lot, about 15 during my career, that were all multi-functional. The last one I did was for the complete version of Goethe's **Faust**, when I constructed two mobile theatres. I was inventing not only the sets but also the situation of the public. We had tribunes on wheels and you could push them around and through the space. You see, the audience should be as near as possible

1

2

ANTHONY AND CLEOPATRA
By William Shakespeare
Salzburg Festival, 1994

1–2 Edith Clever as Cleopatra

1

2

3

FAUST
By J. W. V. Srethe
Berlin, Vienna, 2000/2001

1 Martin Benrath as
   Caesar's ghost
2 Act 4, Robert Hungerbühler
3 Act 2, Hille Beseler, Adam
   Oest, Melanie Blocksdorf
4 Act 5, Bruno Ganz,
   ensemble
5 Act 3, ensemble

to the actor and should see everything so that they can choose what they want to focus on. If you make a Greek tragedy it is better that you have the possibility for the chorus to go into the audience. If you put the chorus on the normal Italian stage then what can you do with it other than go to the right side and then to the left? You see, this is the question and it is a technical one. What is the best situation for the audience to be in for the content and the meaning of the play? For instance, in **Faust** there is a big one-hour carnival. It's better to make the carnival go through the audience, because the carnival is not fixed; the carnival is a pageant and it is moving.

Faust is very special because it is in two parts. The first part is a play that the whole world knows. But this is only a little bit of the whole **Faust**. There is a second part of **Faust** which is double the length of the first part. And this play, nobody can read and nobody can understand. I also couldn't read it even if I understood that it was extremely interesting. So I had to wait until I had enough practice in life and the arts to do this piece. When in 1985 I tried to re-read it I had no problems – I could enter it and enjoy it, and then I started. I wanted to explain all these things that I understood to the actors and

5

4

ORESTAIA
By Aeschylus
Touring production

1 Ensemble, Athens, 1985
2 Elke Petrie as Agamemnon,
  Berlin, 1980

then to ask the actors to transmit this knowledge to the audience. The problem was that nobody wanted to have this show because they said that it was boring and in Germany I am out, they don't want me any more. So I was forced to create my own theatre, get an ensemble together and raise the money.

Once I had my ensemble the preparation work was a very long period of intellectual explanation of the text and general exercises to get unity out of 30 people who were forming a chorus. The next step was how to cope with the language because this language was rhymed verse all the way through and actors today are not used to speaking rhymed verse. We had to learn how to accent it and how to cope with rhyme endings and the highly complicated poetic structure. We had to develop the richness of the space and the movement. We started to run around in an open space, 30 to 40 metres, to orientate ourselves.

We rehearsed for a year as it was the equivalent of six plays and this created enormous frustrations so we had to invent things to help us. We created social events, concerts, singing, things that were not actually to do with the show. The tension and the expectation were very high from everybody because we worked for so long. When the première came we didn't know how to organise the whole thing because the public stayed for nearly two days and the actors needed to take care of them. They took them from one theatre to another and sometimes even ate with them. To organise this was a certain kind of socialisation.

The same problems occurred with **Orestaia** because that was nine hours long. This was a show I was very proud of because with **Orestaia**, even more than with **Faust**, I could use all my 'skills'. I had studied for ten years – History of Art, German Literature, Archaeology and Ancient Greek – and I could use this to make my own translation and get deep into the text. I made it clear from the beginning that there was a directness of speech needed plus a certain height of euphoria that was precisely taken from the Greek original. And so the actors playing the protagonists had a certain freedom to do what they wanted as long as they could read me the text as a kind of a manifesto. Then slowly we also introduced emotion into that. The main work was on the chorus for which I chose a technique. I had 12 choristers, the classical number, and they each had a certain personal

3

HAMLET
By William Shakespeare
Army Theatre, Moscow,
Russia, 1998

3 The grave scene with
   Jeugenig Mironov as
   Hamlet

2

identity and a certain part of the chorus text. They then also joined in occasionally with others in order to underline certain words or phrases.

I never try to unify the acting style, absolutely not, because I am dependent on the actors. If they do not do something then I cannot propose anything. I cannot say, 'please do this or do that'. Perhaps because of my laziness or stupidity, I like to say, 'OK we spoke a lot, we tried to understand, we made a theory, now you go on and please start.' And then they start and all of a sudden it's totally different. And so the actor must do the first step. Then I can see and listen and start to discuss, describe what he did and what effect it made. So I behave as a highly professional, over-paid spectator. This is what I prefer. The most important thing is that at the end the people do not see where the director intervened, that the traces of the directing process are eliminated. The actor must be absolutely dominant on stage, giving the illusion that he invented not only the mise-en-scène and his own behaviour but also that he invented the text.

It's clear that by becoming old the impulse to go on is weakening. I cannot use my body as strongly as I did before. I like very much to make physical activity on stage together with the actors. Also, I must say that the repetitive problems of getting the money etc. are very boring, so I'm looking for changes. I would like to stay at home more so I am constructing a big rehearsal room of 20 to 30 metres in which I will perhaps make productions and I am also teaching. But I am not dependent on anyone. I never have been and that's partly what people hate about me.

I believe that in its present form the theatre will die. Not totally, because it will then go on in other forms, where perhaps we cannot call it theatre any more. Our present living style is about making everything easy and smooth so that even if you are standing with your toothbrush in your mouth you can already switch from 70 different channels. We are developing very short intellectual and artistic breath; we want to do everything now and are very quickly bored. This is all against theatre. Theatre is about offering time, closing the door, blocking the daylight out, and concentrating for three or four hours, in one situation.

JULIUS CAESAR
By William Shakespeare
Salzburg Festspielhaus,
Salzburg, Austria, 1992

1 (pp 116–117) Martin
  Benrath and Gerd Voss
2 Martin Benrath and
  Gerd Voss
3 Thomas Holzman and
  Gerd Voss

3

"It's like this — the theatre sort of gets you — once you're attached that's it."

HABIB
TANVIR

Habib Tanvir is a greatly respected contributor to Indian Theatre. He is a journalist, a dramatist, a poet and director of the Naya Theatre Company which he founded in 1959. His work is a fusion of Indian traditional theatre and the Western influences he acquired from his training in the UK and his extensive travelling. Music is always an important factor in his work, as well as visual imaginative story telling. His company, based in Bhopal in India, has been together since it was formed; some say they are more of a community than a theatre company. Habib Tanvir is also a major political figure; he was a Member of Parliament for six years and is still very involved in political activity to improve the future for the people of India.

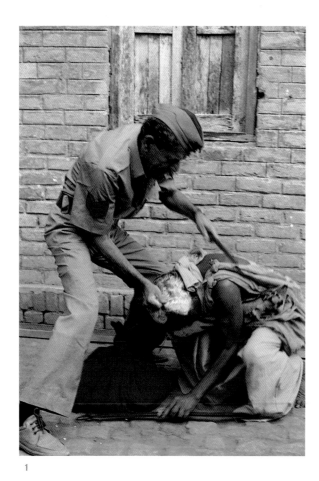

1

HABIB TANVIR: Directing was more or less forced on me to begin with. I was an actor in Bombay at the Indian People's Theatre Association (IPTA), a movement that had grown up in the 1940s opposing British rule, when all my elders, the organisers and directors, were hauled up by the police and taken to jail. We were campaigning for peace, workers' wages, many, many things. After a few days they sent word from inside the jail that I should take over and run the group. So I began writing, organising and directing. I was very young at the time.

In 1954 I moved to Delhi, having lived in Bombay for nine years. I was not making any money out of theatre which I loved above all. It meant sacrifice and hardship so whatever offer came to me to act in films – which I detested at that time – I had to accept. I went to Delhi because I thought if I was out of the way of temptation I would be able to devote myself to theatre and make a professional theatre company, which is what I ultimately did. But not without a very long struggle.

I went to England in 1955 and trained at RADA for a year and then at the Bristol Old Vic Theatre School. I owe much to Richard Ainley and Duncan Ross at the Old Vic. Duncan Ross told me that a production should tell a story and that if you're not bound by tradition you are free. You can have the most beautiful lighting, costumes and sets but if that gets in the way of telling the story then get rid of it.

I then travelled all over Europe for a year observing all kinds of theatre. I learnt a lot. On my return to India I went to Raipur in central India where I belong, to meet my sisters and my mother. There in Raipur one evening I found myself strolling to a maidan near my old school where a play was going on. It was in the Nacha style of theatre – a secular drama typical to that region, performed by the villagers in a dialect called Chattisgarhi, a very sweet language. They are very good actors, musically rich, especially in comedy and satire and lampoons and things of that kind. They can play straight, deadpan and tongue-in-cheek, and make you roar with laughter. I found myself staying there all night watching these actors; they were so fascinating. In the morning I approached them and asked them if they would like to join me in Delhi. Six of them came. Most could not read or write but they were great actors.

Charan Das Chor Charan Das has a guru who insists that he takes five vows: never to eat off a golden plate; never to marry a queen; never to be king; never to ride on an elephant in a procession in his honour and never to lie. Everyone else in the story is corrupt: the policeman takes bribes; the guru extorts money; the treasurer steals golden coins and lies to the queen; and the queen herself tells a lie. Only Charan Das sticks to his vows and in the process gets killed.

CHARAN DAS CHOR
A Rajasthani folk tale recorded by Vijay Dandetha and adapted by Habib Tanvir
Athens, Greece, 1994

1 Habib Tanvir as the blundering policeman and Bhulwa Ram Nadav as the sadhu
2 Panthi dancers of Durg in a ritualistic death dance
3 Bhulwa Ram Yadav as the deceitful and greedy sadhu

3   2

HIRMA KI AMAR KAHANI
Devised by Habib Tanvir
Narainpur, India, 1986

1–2 Narainpur tribal dancers
in rehearsal

In the beginning I got them to act in Hindi but something was lost. Whenever I went back to the villages and saw them there in their own setting they were spellbinding so I gave them the liberty to use their own language. I was experimenting, really, for three years. The work went down well but only with a small number of people. In 1973 I had a breakthrough. I organised a one-month workshop in Raipur and with very many folk artists. The end result was a collage of three Nacha stock comedies called **Gaon Ke Naam Sasural Mor Naam Damad**. People thronged to see that for the first time and it went on and on, show after show. And then the next year was **Charan Das Chor**. So I had more or less got a grip over how to forget my learning and go ahead with improvisational techniques. It was not pure Nacha style but there were elements of it combined with my observations and knowledge of tunes from other parts of India and from all over the world. In the end what I got was a kind of theatre with my signature very vividly imprinted on it. My quest was to do theatre which will be considered very specific so that people from out of India will watch it and say, 'well, it's theatre all right but if we were to try we couldn't do it quite that way.' I think I had discovered by then that universality of art has to go through specificity – through particularity to the universal and not the other way round.

I was mixing the Chattisgarhi village actors with urban, middle class educated actors and not very successfully. It looked like a patchwork. Either the villagers dominated and actually swallowed the urban actor, or the urban actor, in trying to seek space for himself on the stage, would marginalise the folk actor. However, now I am able to produce a blend of the two, and I do bilingual written theatre, in Chattisgarhi and Hindi. I'm comfortable with this and the actors also seem comfortable.

Improvisation is one big method by which I try out even a written text before throwing it into the process of rehearsals. Sometimes it is a folk tale and I just get actors to improvise and if it is dull we will discuss it and see if they could improve it. Then I run to my desk and get down to writing. There are some other methods, but when directing a play in the main I use improvisation. I don't tell them where to go and what to do because it is not in their tradition. Those who can will read, but those who can't are given the lines by the others. They get familiar with it once or twice and then I make them get up and improvise and forget all about the text.

1

2

4

5

DEKH RAHEY HAIN NAIN
Based on *Virat*, a story by
Stefan Zweig; adapted by
Habib Tanvir
Sri Ram Centre, Delhi, India,
1992

3 Bulwa Ram Yadav,
   Nageen Tanvir and Brij Lal
   Lenjvar performing a ritual
4–5 Deepak Tiwari and Chait
   Ram Yadav as the
   two brothers
6 The last scene
   (pp126–127): a ritualistic
   dance by the Mandla
   dancers of the Gond tribe

Dekh Rahey Hain Nain In this adapted folk
tale, Virat accidentally kills his brother in war.
His dead brother's eyes haunt him all his life,
determining all his actions, even his own
death. Virat then relinquishes the sword and
is granted land and a luxurious house by the
King. He is happy until he is confronted by
his dead brother's accusing eyes in one of his
slaves in a subsequent sequence; thus the
same actor plays many roles including that
of a woman. Virat continues to recognise his
brother's haunting eyes in others throughout
the story and seeks emancipation from the
King by doing the lowest possible job, that
of burning dead bodies.

When they get back to the text the illiterate actors quite often arrive much earlier than the educated ones; their hearing and memorising gets so sharpened.

We generally rehearse for a month or two months but there have been occasions, at least with one play, where I have taken almost two years. That's not rehearsing regularly every day but toying with the play and with the idea and then getting some improvisations done and then often feeling dissatisfied by something very essential to the play, the characterisation or the plot. Sometimes it's a production difficulty like the experience I had with a particular show **Bahadur Kalarin**, an oral tale very popular with the villagers. Bahadur, a very beautiful wine-seller, lived with her son and looked after him with great affection. Her wine became famous and she earned a lot of money and respect and got her son married nicely. But the boy was not satisfied and wanted to marry again. So again he married and a third time till he had married 126 times. Finally he discovered that he was really in love with his mother. She was shocked. She then treated him to a very rich meal and asked all the women of the household and all the villagers not to supply him with water. The food was hot and greasy and he was very, very thirsty. The mother said, 'there is no water in the house at all today; you can go to the well yourself and draw some.' And as he went to the well she pushed him in and killed him and then killed herself.

My stumbling block was that improvisation was giving me black-and-white pictures. The actors were tending to make the son into a villainous, womanising rascal and the woman into an angel. I said this was not acceptable. I wanted to see greys. So I put it to them that the son may not be the only guilty party – the mother may have some share in it. I said, 'Perhaps you find incest something quite alien – you are probably not aware of this kind of relationship? Or are you?' And then suddenly, one, two, three… many, many stories were told by the villager actors. Stories of sister and brother, uncle and niece, father and daughter, and so on and so forth. Recently in fact they had heard a rumour of a mother and son living together. I said the rumour is enough. It may be false but if the public mind produces the rumour and in fact they are together, maybe innocently, that rumour has some substance – if not in relation to the truth then in regard to the reality of their psychology, to their imaginations. That reality is more important for us. So they agreed. And supposing this

BAHADUR KALARIN
Adapted by Habib Tanvir
Lyric Theatre, London, UK,
1983 (1, 2) and All India Fine
Arts Auditorium, Delhi, India,
1978 (3)

1 Mandla dancers from the
   Gond tribe, Madhya
   Pradesh, India
2 Fida Markam as Bahadur
   and Ram Charan Nirmalkar
   as her neighbour
3 Fida Markam

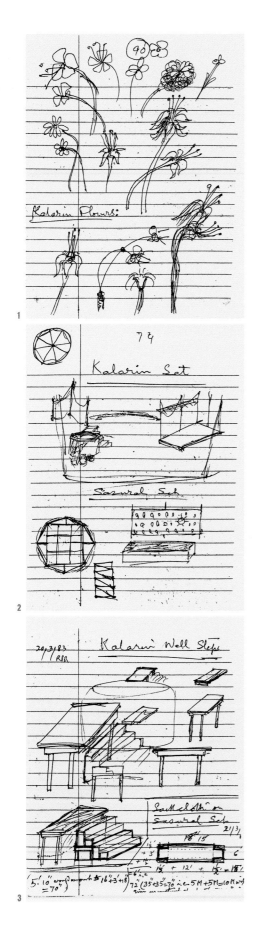

1

2

3

woman, this Bahadur, was drooling over the son and fondling him and pampering him and bathing him with her own hands till a great age and letting him sleep by her side till he was 13, and he wetting the bed. And she would massage his body with oil and comb the hair and dress him up and he being the only male figure in the house. That can produce a kind of disease in the boy, a kind of fixation.

He doesn't enjoy any other woman and then suddenly realises his mother has only to touch his head and ruffle his hair and he gets aroused as a man. So that could be a discovery for him, and then he simply declares the truth to his mother, 'I have seen so many women, but none like you.' This is exactly what he said to her. When I said that to my actress Fida Markam she brought great delicate handling to the situation and the actor who was to be the son also brought those nuances, and then I began to get greys. The previous improvisations got me nowhere but after this intervention we went galloping with the play. And actually I love that play the most because it was extremely rewarding. We got the results with such good actors doing it.

Despite the dominance of cinema and TV I see a bright future for theatre. Electronic media have taken over temporarily but theatre has very deep roots, especially street theatre. There are still many, many young people out there who are struggling to make good theatre. It's like this – the theatre sort of gets you – once you're attached that's it.

BAHADUR KALARIN
Adapted by Habib Tanvir
Birla Theatre, Kolkata,
India, 1978

1 Sketch of flower designs
  for the last scene
2 Sketch of the set including
  the well (top and bottom)
  and steps
3 Sketch of the steps
4 Mandla dancers from the
  Gond tribe singing and
  dancing about the
  intransience of life
5 The witch-doctor divines
  the need for a third bride
  for Bahadur's son

1

2

BASANT RITU KA SAPNA (A MIDSUMMER NIGHT'S DREAM)
By William Shakespeare
Lady Shri Ram College lawn
and auditorium, Delhi, India,
1992 and 1990

1 Dancers of the Muria tribe
  as spirits casting Oberon's
  spell on Titania
2 Fairies with Bottom and
  Titania
3 Oberon with fairies
4 The last scene: Thisby
  committing suicide after
  the death of Pyramus
5 Titania with the fairies

3

4

5

JULIE TAYMOR

Julie Taymor is a director of theatre, opera and film and a designer of costumes, sets, masks and puppets. In the mid-seventies she was awarded a Watson Fellowship to study theatre and puppetry in Eastern Europe and Asia which enabled her to spend four years in Indonesia. She was deeply inspired by Indonesian theatrical traditions, their use of puppets and masks and the role that theatre played in their society. She continues to draw on these experiences, as well as influences from Africa, Japan, Europe and Mexico in her work. Taymor rose to international fame when she created **The Lion King** on Broadway, using her unique style of story telling – a high-tech, low-tech approach to the production. She says that the forms she works with are as old as theatre itself. Portions of this article were republished from *Julie Taymor: Playing With Fire* by permission of Harry N. Abrams.

JULIE TAYMOR: My first exploration into non-traditional theatre began when I joined the Theatre Workshop of Boston at age 15. It was the sixties, when people were tossing out the playwright and starting to create theatre from improvisations of the ensemble. This was the era of the Open Theatre, the Living Theatre, Herbert Blau and Peter Brook. My experience at the Workshop was tremendous because it was the first time, as a performer, that I was also responsible for the content. This total approach to the creation of a theatre work continued once I joined Herbert Blau's group at Oberlin College. The company was a mixed group of professionals and students, and I was the youngest member. We created work from a concept, an idea. For instance, we developed a piece called **The Donner Party** which was about the 19th-century gold rush to the west coast of the United States. We conjured the work through newspaper clippings, diaries, novels and through our imagination. This was an enormous opening for me as a creator – especially visually. The entire **Donner Party** was performed within the physical structure of an American square dance – a concept that I brought to the table.

Prior to Oberlin I had been to Paris, at age 16, to attend L'École de Mime Jacques Lecoq. There, I studied mime and masks, and was first introduced to the power of abstract puppetry. We would look at the shapes of objects and try to discover their inherent character: How would a broom move, walk? What would its personality be? We explored the essences of objects, the very nature of matter, the physicality of colour, the elements, emotion etc. This process was the introduction to the concept of ideographs.

The Tempest provided Taymor with an ideal opportunity to match a heightened physicality of the performance with the elevated poetry of Shakespeare's language. Taymor divided the costumes for her production into four symbolic categories: natural, supernatural, court and clown. The costumes of Prospero, Miranda and Ferdinand were the most timeless and natural. For the monster Caliban, on the other hand, the masks of the Mud Men of New Guinea came to Taymor's mind, and she designed a 'rocklike' mask with only two eye holes, mouth and ear holes for detail. For the first third of the play Caliban is masked, but when he thinks he has been liberated by the clowns, a transformation occurs. In drunken exaltation he splits open his rock head with a log and, as in birth, his face is finally revealed.

THE TEMPEST
By William Shakespeare
Directed by Julie Taymor;
music by Elliot Goldenthal;
puppetry and masks by
Julie Taymor
Produced by Theatre for
a New Audience at CSC
(Classic Stage Company),
New York, USA, 1986

1 Peter Callendar as Caliban
  with Robert Strattel as
  Prospero and Freda Foh
  Stien as Miranda
2 Avery Brooks as Caliban

1

1

2

3

4

5

6

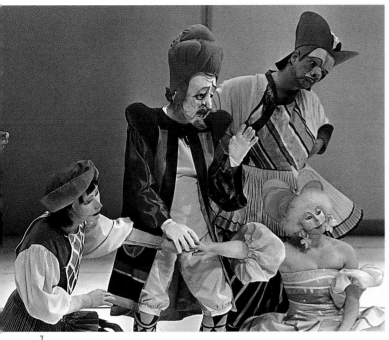

The King Stag, an oriental fantasy from the 18th century, was written in the tradition of the commedia dell'arte by Carlo Gozzi. The characters include the stock commedia characters such as Pantalone, the old Buffoon, Harlequin, Deramo, the romantically noble king, and Tartaglia, the evil Prime Minister. In addition to the human elements there is an array of animals and magical events in the play. Taymor created a unifying style for all these elements that would blend Eastern and Western techniques and visual motifs. On the first day of rehearsal Taymor had half masks ready, as they were to inform the actors in their characterisation as much as the dialogue. Similarly, the costumes were designed to be as sculptured as the masks, as they represented the core of the characters themselves. All the costumes were made of white fabric and each was individually half hand-dyed, painted or stencilled. The stags were constructed out of stencilled silk stretched on shaped rattan frames whose moving parts were pulled by the strings of the visible puppeteer.

THE KING STAG
By Carlo Gozzi
Directed by Andrei Serban;
music by Elliot Goldenthal;
costumes, masks, puppetry
and choreography by
Julie Taymor

1–6 Costume designs by
Taymor: Deramo; Tartaglia;
Clarice; Pantalone;
Truffaldino; Leandro
7 Christopher Moore as
Leandro, Jeremy Geidt
as Pantalone, Harry S.
Murphy as Brighella,
Lynn Chausow as Clarice
8 Thomas Derrah as King
Deramo and Richard
Grussin as Tartaglia

7

8

JUAN DARIÉN: A CARNIVAL MASS
Based on a short story by
Horacio Quiroga; adapted
by Julie Taymor and Elliot
Goldenthal
Directed by Julie Taymor;
music by Eliot Goldenthal;
sets and costumes by G. W.
Mercier and Julie Taymor
Lincoln Center Theater,
Lincoln, USA, in association
with Music Theater Group,
1996–7

1 Drawing by Taymor:
   Señor Toledo,
   the teacher
2 Señor Toledo and
   the school

JULIE TAYMOR

1

An ideograph can be best explained by comparing it to a
Japanese brush painting where with just three brush strokes
you express the entire bamboo forest. You alleviate yourself
from the details and cornice work and you go for the essence
of the abstraction. An ideograph can be useful in probing
the larger concept for a piece but also, when I make masks,
I start by looking for the ideograph of a character. As a
maskmaker you only have one stroke, one fixed sculpture to
say it all about a character. You have to be able to do it within
a few shapes, lines and forms. Take Mufasa from **The Lion
King**; the essence of his character is found in his symmetry,
in his solid, balanced nature – he embodies a benevolent
wholeness like the sun. So for his mask, his mane encircles
his face and radiates outward in the image of the sun.
Now Scar is about asymmetry and angles, more like an
unpredictable snake. Jagged, serpentine lines shape the
visual ideograph for the mask of his character and that
in turn informs the actors how to move, what their body
language should be. Another example is to take **The Lion
King** script and ask what is the fundamental ideograph for
the whole story? It's obviously the circle – 'the Circle of Life'

1

JUAN DARIÉN: A CARNIVAL MASS
Based on a short story by
Horacio Quiroga; adapted
by Julie Taymor and Elliot
Goldenthal
Directed by Julie Taymor;
sets and costumes by G. W.
Mercier and Julie Taymor
Lincoln Center Theater,
Lincoln, USA, in association
with Music Theater Group,
1996–7

1   Production photo: the
    hunter and the mother
2   Sculpture: plague victim
    sculpture by Taymor
3   Drawing: the mother
    by Taymor
4   Sketch: the hunter
    by Taymor

Juan Darién: A Carnival Mass This South
American story of compassion and revenge
enabled Taymor to explore a multitude of
puppetry techniques. Using imagery and
music as the principal storytellers, Taymor
and her long-time collaborator, composer
Elliot Goldenthal, created an original Passion
play with a Latin Requiem Mass serving as
the text. The juxtaposition of live actor and
puppet was one of the key emotional and
humanising factors of the drama. The main
character of Juan transformed five times: first
he appears as a jaguar cub (rod-and-string
puppet); next as an infant (hand-manipulated
doll); at age ten he changes into a four-foot-
tall Bunraku puppet; and upon the death of
his mother he becomes a flesh-and-blood
boy. From this point on, Juan was the only
human (unmasked) actor in the play. The final
transformation occurred when the child,
suspected of being a jaguar, is burned alive
on the Bengal lights (fireworks, scaffolding).
The nine-foot-tall schoolteacher, Señor Toledo,
had an open book for hair with pages that
fluttered when he was angry. His schoolroom
was a Punch-and-Judy-type walking stage
supported by three puppeteers who also
manipulated six finger-puppets of raucous
children, including Juan.

2

3

4

1

– and it becomes the major symbol for the piece. You then take this image to your designers and look for where it can repeat itself as a motif, like a melody in a symphony that echoes through the piece.

The way that I would begin rehearsals is by reading the text as in any normal rehearsal. But before beginning the actual scene work I would start by asking the company, 'what's this play about? If you could pick one theme that represents the play what would it be? Violence, for example. How do you express violence? Give me a physical image for violence.' In this way, we would open up the play in a free-wheeling, imaginative way before grounding ourselves in the formality of the text. It helps to do this first without words, because words use a logical part of your brain and often overpower the visceral expression. This process of challenging the actor to take the entire play and put it into a beginning, a middle and an end – an ideograph – with just a few brush strokes, is incredibly productive.

When I directed **The Transposed Heads**, an adaptation of the novella by Thomas Mann, the actors discovered an extraordinary ideograph in rehearsal. The story is about the tension between friendship, love and jealousy. The two men tried to express in a physical image the nature of their camaraderie. They put their four feet together, side by side but facing opposite directions. Then they linked their right arms, clasped hands and leaned backwards. They had formed an upside-down triangle, made out of a delicate balance that was dependent on the mutual support of both men. The image was not only a triangle, but also a heart. Subtle, perhaps subliminal, but a profound gesture that would be idiosyncratic to those two characters while also reflecting the entire essence of the piece.

Anthony Hopkins often uses ideographs in his work, perhaps unconsciously. One example would be the hand gesture in *Howard's End*. There's an incredible moment where his hand comes up to his face, it's just a gesture – very Hopkins – but it's an ideograph because it's something so specific to that character that also says so much more than just 'stop'. When I worked with him on my film *Titus*, we looked for these moments. Even with a film – which is a much more literal medium than the theatre – one begins to unravel its mystery by narrowing down the themes. In *Titus*, hands were a recurring image. Hands get lopped off; hands bestow power

Fool's Fire reveals how Taymor's highly visual and stylised approach can adapt well to the medium of film. Edgar Allan Poe's black comedy of revenge was an ideal vehicle for exploring grotesque and extraordinary characterisation. The story tells of the capture of a dwarf, Hop-Frog, who is forced to play court jester to a tyrannical king and equally despised ministers. The dwarf's part as principal character and his (ironic) dehumanisation within the story is heightened by his being the only actor within a cast of 'monstrous' Boschlike puppets.

FOOL'S FIRE
Screenplay by Julie Taymor, based on the short story 'Hop Frog' by Edgar Allan Poe Directed by Julie Taymor; original music by Elliot Goldenthal; costume and character design by Julie Taymor

1 Sketches for the main characters by Julie Taymor
2 The Banquet

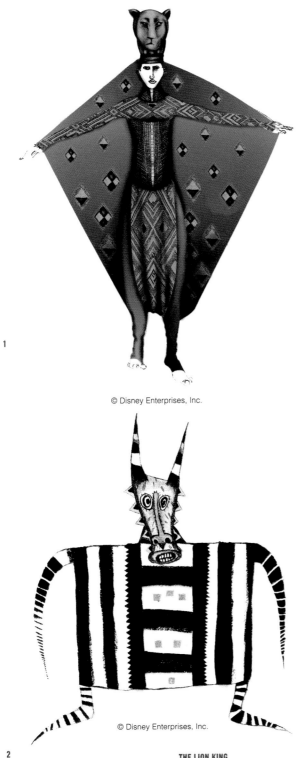

1

© Disney Enterprises, Inc.

2

© Disney Enterprises, Inc.

THE LION KING
Directed by Julie Taymor;
costumes, masks, puppetry
by Julie Taymor
New Amsterdam Theater,
New York, USA, 2000

1–3 Sketches for dancing
lioness, trickster and hyena
by Taymor © Disney
Enterprises, Inc.

and misuse it. These ideas come from the language – you're
not laying them on the text, they're in the text, especially
with a writer as profound and as visual as Shakespeare.

Film is often a more 'realistic' medium and has different
requirements than the theatre. It's very different when one is
asked to wear a mask and through it to find their character
and movement. When we were working on **The Green Bird**
we did commedia dell' arte workshops to free up the actors
and help them establish the world of their characters. The
casting process is an important gauge of how free an actor
is to do the kind of work required in a mask drama. When
the actors came in to audition for **The Green Bird** they first
read the text as in a normal audition. Then I gave each actor
three different masks, having nothing to do with the play.
After some private time before a mirror each actor, one at
a time, would come back into the room and improvise with
each of those masks. I was not just looking to see how
they could play the part, but how game they were in the
art of improvisation.

My work is often very hard to categorise. It's tiring to watch
people try to label what kind of theatre I do, what kind of
artist I am. My productions such as **Juan Darién**, or even
The Green Bird, don't fall within standard expectations of a
form so it's very hard for people to know what they're going
to get. People go to the theatre with certain expectations and
it's wonderful when you can give people what they don't even
know they want. Sometimes I walk into a theatre, look at a
particular set and think, 'Oh God, I'm going to be sitting in
a living room for the next two hours.' That is the death of
theatre – when you already know what you're going to get
from the onset. It's not that you need to create a circus that
is constantly changing, but you have to challenge the
audience's expectations. Break down those boundaries.
You can do anything you like as long as you do it well.

The Lion King Taymor relished the challenge of bringing one of the most popular films in recent history to the stage. Her first task was to not only expand the 'Lion King' story but also to determine the placement of new songs and choreography, setting the overall concept that would guide the production's visual aesthetic. The dominant theme that emerged was the circle – 'the Circle of Life'. And Taymor's bold use of what she calls 'the double event' allows the audience to experience the dualities of puppet/actor and human/animal. Her stylisation demands that the audience fill in the blanks, making them complicit with the artist in the creative act. The show has achieved international success on stages in New York, Los Angeles, Toronto, Japan and London.

© Disney Enterprises, Inc.

JULIE TAYMOR

147

3

1

2

3

FRIDA
Directed by Julie Taymor
Miramax, 2002

1 Salma Hayek as Frida
Kahlo and Alfred Molina
as Diego Rivera
2 Antonio Banderas, Salma
Hayek, Ashley Judd and
Alfred Molina
3 Salma Hayek

Taymor's extensive abilities have also led to
success in film directing. **Frida** (1–3) tells the
story of Frida Kahlo and her husband Diego
Rivera, the larger-than-life painters who
became perhaps the most acclaimed artists
in Mexican history, and whose tempestuous
love affair, landmark journeys to America and
outrageous personalities made them
legendary. **Oedipus Rex** (5) was also
produced as a film which premièred at the
Sundance Film Festival, Park City, Utah, 1993

OEDIPUS REX
Composed by Igor Stravinsky;
libretto by Jean Cocteau
Live opera production and
film directed by Julie Taymor
Saito Kinen Festival,
Matsumoto, Japan, 1992

5 Jessye Norman as Jocasta

TITUS
Directed by Julie Taymor
Clear Blue Sky Productions
and Fox Searchlight, 1999

4 Taymor and Antony
Hopkins confer
between takes of the
crossroads scene

4

"With movement we start with stillness"

ROBERT WILSON

Born in Texas, Robert Wilson trained as an architect at Brooklyn's Pratt Institute. He studied painting with George McMeil in Paris and later worked with architect Paola Solari in Arizona. In 1968 Wilson gathered a group of artists together in New York and formed the Byrd Hoffman School of Byrds who performed in a loft building in Manhattan. In 1969 two major Wilson productions appeared in New York city: **The King of Spain** and **The Life and Times of Sigmund Freud**. Wilson received international acclaim in 1971 for **The Deafman Glance**, a silent opera created in collaboration with Raymond Andrews, a deaf-mute boy whom Wilson adopted. After the Paris première, French surrealist Louis Artagon wrote, 'He is what we, from whom surrealism was born, dreamed would come after us and go beyond us.' Wilson has since become one of the most prolific and innovative directors of our time.

The Deafman Glance lasted seven hours and was what Wilson termed a 'silent opera'. Raymond Andrews, the young, deaf-mute boy whom Wilson had adopted, had told him a story about a cow who swallowed the sun, which made her head fall off. Wilson was deeply moved by this story and saw it as one of great universality, and it became the beginning of his idea for **The Deafman Glance**. The show was a tour de force featuring extraordinary backdrops and scenery by Fred Kalo. The forest setting filled every inch of the stage with detail and movement that unfolded and transformed itself over the course of the show.

.

THE DEAFMAN GLANCE
By Robert Wilson
Brooklyn Academy of Music
Performance, New York,
USA, 1971

1 Raymond Andrews
2 Ensemble

ROBERT WILSON: When I grew up in Texas I didn't have an opportunity to see very much theatre. I had never been to the opera, I never went to art galleries or to museums and it was not until I moved to New York in my early twenties that I first really went to the theatre. I went to see Broadway plays and I didn't like them. I still don't for the most part, and I went to the opera and I didn't like that either and I still don't for the most part. And then I went to see the work of George Balanchine and I liked that very much. I liked it because it was classically constructed. I liked the formality of it and I liked the distance the dancer had with the way he presented himself in front of a public. I particularly liked the abstract ballets that he made with the music of Stravinsky. This was a kind of mental space that I didn't see or hear in the Broadway theatre or in the opera. I liked it because it was not psychological; it was not burdened with naturalism, all of which seems to me to be about a lie on stage – it's not natural, it's something artificial. Then I saw the work of Ms Cunningham with John Cage. I liked that very much for the same reasons that I liked Balanchine's work. What was

1

particularly interesting with Cunningham and Cage was how they constructed what I was hearing and seeing; it could often be a counterpoint, and in this dualism they could reinforce one another without having to illustrate or decorate. I have an aversion to this horrible decoration that we see on stage in theatre and in opera. You know, they should burn all these theatre schools that teach theatre decoration. Theatre should be architectural; it started out being architectural and then it got to be something else.

I did not study theatre and if I had I would not be making the theatre I am making now. I studied business administration in a pre-law programme at the University of Texas. I studied painting and architecture at New York and I was greatly influenced by Daniel Stern, Head of the Department of Psychology at Columbia University, and studies he was doing

DEATH, DESTRUCTION & DETROIT III
Devised by Robert Wilson;
text by Umberto Eco; music
by Ryuchi Sakamoto
Teatro Communale, Modena,
Italy, 1999

1 Over (pp154–155)

1

with the body language between mothers and infants. I came to theatre really because I had adopted a 13-year-old Afro-American boy who had never been to school and knew no words, and saw and understood the world through visual signs and signals. We ended up making some small works in the theatre together that eventually became a seven-hour play called **The Deafman Glance** and much to my surprise it was a huge success. Those were the influences on the work I'm doing today and those still are the roots.

I usually start rehearsals in stillness and with silence. John Cage said there's no such thing as silence. For instance, if we begin to speak or sing or to hear a violin play it only continues the sound we're already hearing; so it doesn't begin and it doesn't end when we stop playing the violin or stop singing or stop speaking because if I'm listening there's always a continuum of sound. So it's one line, one thing. With movement we start with stillness. Martha Graham said there's no such thing as no movement – there's always movement, so as long as we're alive we're moving, but in stillness we become aware of the movement that is within us. And then when we move outwardly, the line just continues. So I usually start that way. I start with an empty space and then I put something in that space and see what happens. And then I work either separately or at the same time in putting in the audio score with what I'm seeing; it's not placed by chance with what you're hearing, it's consciously constructed.

I think about light from the beginning. For me the light is the most important element in theatre because it helps us to hear and see which are the primary ways in which we relate to one another. So without light there's no space. In a piece like **Einstein on the Beach** it's so structural, it's like a primary participant. Here, light is architectural; it's a part of a book that is written; it's not something that is thought about afterwards. André Malraux said after the war that the dilemma of Western drama and opera is that we have been bound by literature. And I think what he meant is that our primary concern is the text and what we're hearing so that the visual book for theatre has always been a second thing to what we are hearing and seeing. If we look at other parts of the world, if we look at China, or Japan, or Indonesia, India, Africa, Latin America, the Eskimos, the north-west-coast Indians, this is something completely different. Their visual books for theatre are considered and learned at the same time as an audio score is. If you're a singer in the Peking

1 THE BLACK RIDER
Devised by Robert Wilson;
text by William Burroughs;
music by Tom Waits
Theatre du Chatelet, Paris,
France, 1990

Black Rider is Wilson's homage to German Expressionism with the distorted perspectives of Expressionist painting and the exaggerated gestures of cabaret and silent films. It was loosely based on the German folk tale underlying Von Weber's opera **Der Freischutz**. Wilson had the idea that there would be indoor scenes and outdoor scenes and that the two would alternate. This picture (1) is taken from Scene 10, the crossroads scene. It is a forest, the trees are hanging upside down. Wilhelm is frightened; the dead mother appears and then the devil flies in on a chair and sings like a gospel preacher.

2–3 ALCESTE
By Christoph Willibald Gluck
Lyric Opera, Chicago,
USA, 1990

4 O CORVO BRANCO (WHITE RAVEN)
Madrid, 1998
Over (pp158–159)

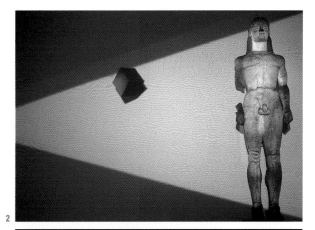

2

3

Opera you learn to stand, how to move the sleeve of your
costume when you're aged two, and there are hundreds of
different ways of moving that sleeve. If you're a Noh actor in
Japan you learn how to walk on stage at age two, and how
to move your hand for weeping or where to place the emotion
deep within yourself or whatever. But in the 14th-century
book on drama there are notations on the look of a stage
and it's something that's been passed down and learned.
If you're in Bolly you learn movements of fingers and of eyes.
Imagine asking a Western opera singer to do a specific eye
movement – they would think you're crazy, but the eyes are
part of a language that is theatrical. Our Western culture has
lost something in terms of developing an adequate visual
book for theatre.

In 30-something years of working I've never, ever told an
actor what to think. And I can't do that. I don't talk about
psychology or interpretation. Sometimes in dramaturgy other
people will do that, but I don't. I give formal directions; I
say 'quicker', 'slower', 'more interior', 'more exterior', 'this line
should be longer', 'more space under your arms', 'quieter',
'louder' – I give direction like that. So they're given a rather
rigid mega-structure for whatever they're doing and they
can bring to it their own fantasies and their own ideas and
imagination. It's a little bit like an architect who builds an
apartment building and you live in the apartment and you like
your room all white and I like mine all red, and someone else
likes something else. We each fill our room the way we want
it, and we all live together in a kind of harmony because we
have this mega-structure of a building with an organisation
and structure to it and we fill in our own personalities in these
apartments. And a good director is like that.

I say to actors, 'you've got your ideas and that's OK but don't
insist on them too much because if you do there's no space
for me to have my own ideas. So you can indicate your
ideas, your feelings and you can express that but have a
respect that I might have something different in mind, and
let's have a dialogue.' Most theatre is too insistent upon an
idea so it's very difficult to have a genuine exchange with
the public, because the actor is there like a bad high-school
teacher, with his mind made up on a fixed idea or an
interpretation, so there's very little space for other ideas.
Theatre is more complicated than that. When Romeo says
he loves Juliet it's very complicated, and perhaps the body
is moving faster than we think but there's a language there.

1 THE MAGIC FLUTE
Music by Wolfgang Amadeus
Mozart
Opera Bastille, Paris, France,
1990

2 KING LEAR
By William Shakespeare
Workshop at UCLA extension,
USA, May 1985

2

1

2

3

4

1 MEMORY LOSS
By Robert Wilson
Venice Biennale, Italy, 1993

2 BLUEBEARD'S CASTLE
By Bela Bartók
Salzburg Festspielhaus,
Salzburg, Austria, 1995

3 THE CIVIL WARS
Devised by Robert Wilson
and Heiner Müller
Loeb Drama Center,
Cambridge, Massachusetts,
USA, 1985

4 EINSTEIN ON THE BEACH
Devised by Robert Wilson;
music by Philip Glass
Théâtre Munipal, Avignon,
France, 1976

Memory Loss Inspired by a letter from Heiner Muller, Wilson's installation contained a wax bust (cast from Wilson's own head and shoulders) as the centrepiece of a vast architectural poem.

Bluebeard's Castle was paired with Schonberg's **Erwartung** at the Festspielhaus, Salzburg Festival, in 1995.

The Civil Wars Perhaps Wilson's most ambitious project, this multi-national epic had individual sections developed in Japan, United States, France, the Netherlands, Germany and Italy. The show was originally created as part of the Olympic Arts Festival to be held in conjunction with the Olympic games in LA in 1984. However, the Olympic committee cancelled the engagement and only four sections were ever performed: the Netherlands, Germany, Italy and the United States, for which Wilson received widespread acclaim.

Einstein on the Beach An innovative approach to musical theatre, the work represented a move away from the complex mise en scène of his earlier plays towards a more stripped-down geometry. There were three visual themes that repeated themselves three times; a court of justice, a train, and a spaceship hovering over a field.

Ka Mountain and Gardenia Terrace Wilson subtitled this production 'a story about a family and some people changing.' It was a vast and complex piece involving hundreds of performers and lasting seven full days.

5 KA MOUNTAIN AND
GARDENIA TERRACE
By Robert Wilson, Andrew de
Groat, Cynthia Lubar, James
Neu, Ann Wilson, Mel
Andringa and others
Haft Tan Mountain (Shiraz-
Persepolis Festival of the Arts)
Shiraz, Iran, 1972

Whether it's a news broadcaster on TV giving a blank report of the number of people killed in the Middle East in a suicide attack – if you break down the sound of his voice, the gesture, the movements, it's very complicated what's going on. For us to assume that we can fully comprehend whatever we're doing is not possible, so an intelligent person will have some distance.

I learnt a **Hamlet** speech when I was 12 and I have said it many times; every time I say it I can think about it completely differently. That's not to say that it does not have meaning – it's full of meaning – but to narrow it down to one idea limits the possibility of all the other ideas. Shakespeare didn't completely understand what he wrote, it's too complex; it's full of ideas and it's something that is cosmic. Each time we think about it we can think about it in very different ways and that's what's rich about it. So keep open, that's what I say to the actors. It doesn't matter if you're a naturalistic actor or a psychological actor – if you're a good actor you're a good actor, and a good actor will always have a distance and space, a kind of respect for the public.

Theatre must be simple; it must be accessible. The mystery is in the skin, so the skin of the piece must be easily understood. Then beneath the skin you have meat and then you have bones – you have other structures and layers but I think it's important that theatre be about one thing first and then it can be about a million things. So often theatre is too complicated – it should always be simple. We make theatre for the public; that's why we write plays, that's why we direct them, that's why we act in them, that's why we make stage sets for them, costumes, lights, it's for the public. Theatre is needed by man. Man has always had theatre, a place to congregate and have an exchange of ideas – it's inherent in our nature.

Eugenio Barba

1954	Completed Education at The Military Academy of Naples
1960	Went to Norway and studied French and Norwegian Literature and History of Religion at Oslo Universty
1961	Went to Warsaw, Poland, and studied directing at The State Theatre School
1962	Left The State Theatre School to join Jerzy Grotowski at the Teatr 13 Rzedow in Opole
1963	Travelled to India where he discovered Kathakali theatre
1965	First book *In Search of a Lost Theatre* published in Italy and Hungary
1964	Returned to Oslo and created the Odin Teatret
1965	First production **Ornitofilerne** by Jens Bjorneboe shown in Norway, Sweden, Finland and Denmark
1966	Invited by the Danish Municipality of Hostebro to create a theatre laboratory in an old farm
	With Odin Barba has created over 23 productions, some taking two years to prepare. These include:
1969	**Ferai**
1972	**Mins Fars Hus (My Father's House)**
1980	**Brecht's Ashes**
1985	**The Gospel According to Oxyrincus**
1988	**Talabot**
1993	**Kaomos**
1998	**Mythos**
2002	**Salt**

Anne Bogart

1967	Educated at Bard College
1974	Studied at University of New York
1979	Invited to teach at the Experimental Theater Wing; offered time and facilities to grow as a director and enough money to support the downtown theatre work she was producing
1987	Became co-Artistic Director of Via Theater with Brian Jucha
1989–90	Became Artistic Director of Trinity Repertory Theater
1992	Co-founded the SITI Company with Tadashi Suzuki
1992	**Orestes**, Spa Little Theater, Saratoga Springs, New York
1992	**Dionysus**, (Sct and SITI) Bernhard Theater, Saratoga Springs, New York
1993	**The Medium**, Toga Festival, Toga
1993	**Waiting For Romeo**, Bernhard Theater, Saratoga Springs, New York
1994	**The Medium**, New York Theater Workshop, New York
1994	**SmallLives/Big Dreams**, Toga Festival, Bernhard Theater, New York, and Hamilton College, New York
1995	**Small Lives/Big Dreams** and **The Medium**, Modern Masters Festival, Louisville, Kentucky
1995	**The Medium**, Theatre Artaud, San Francisco
1995	**Going, Going, Gone**, Bernhard Theater, New York
1995	Honoured as ATL's first 'Modern Master' as a part of the 1995 Classics in Context Festival, USA
1996	**The Medium**, Out There Festival, Minnisota
1996	**Small Lives/Big Dreams**, Olympic Festival, Atlanta
1997	**Miss Julie**, Actors Theater, Louisville, Kentucky
1997	**Culture of Desire**, City Theater, Pittsburg
1997	**Bob**, Theatre Archa, Prague
1998	**Private Lives**, Actors Theater, Louisville, Kentucky
1998	**Bob**, New York Theater Workshop, New York
1998	**Seven Deadly Sins**, New York City Opera, New York
1998	**Alice's Adventures**, Warner Center for the Arts, Columbus
1999	**Alice's Adventures**, City Stage, Springfield
1999	**Cabin Pressure**, Humana Festival of New American Plays
1999	**War of the Worlds**, (Radio play) Laurie Beechman Theater
2000	**Room**, Wexner, Center for the Arts, Columbus
2000	**Bob**, Contemporary Art Center, Warsaw

Declan Donnellan

1972	Read English and Law at Cambridge, England
1979	Called to the Bar at Middle Temple
1981	Founded Cheek By Jowl with Nick Ormerod Productions include: **Andromache** by Racine; **A Family Affair** by Ostrovsky; **Sarah** by Lessing and **The Cid** by Corneille. He wrote and directed **Lady Betty**, adapted **Vanity Fair** and staged **The Duchess of Malfi**. His productions of Shakespeare include **Twelfth Night**, **A Midsummer Night's Dream**, **Macbeth, Much Ado About Nothing**, **Measure For Measure**, and **As You Like It**.
1989–97	Associate Director of the Royal National Theatre, UK Productions include: **Fuente Ovejuna**; **Peer Gynt**; **Sweeney Todd** and both parts of **Angels in America** by Tony Kushner. Freelance productions include: **Macbeth and Philoctetes**, National Theatre of Finland; **Romeo and Juliet**, New Shakespeare Company, UK; **The School for Scandal**, Royal Shakespeare Company, UK; **Hayfever**, Savoy Theatre, UK; and his own version of **Antigone** by Sophocles at the Old Vic, UK.
1997	**The Winter's Tale** in Russian with The Maly Theatre Company, St. Petersburg
1998	**Le Cid** with French actors at the Festival d'Avignon, France
2001	**Boris Godunuv** created with the Moscow Arts Gorky Theatre, Moscow
2001	**Falstaff**, Salzburg Festspielhaus, Salzburg Festival, Austria
2000–02	**Homebody/Kabul** by Tony Kushner, New York Theater Workshop, and The Young Vic, London

William Kentridge

1976	Graduated from University of the Witwatersand
1976–78	Student at Johannesburg Art Foundation
1982–02	Kentridge's theatre productions created in association with the Handspring Puppet Company are:
1982	**Woyzeck on the Highveld**
1995	**Faustus in Africa!**
1997	**Ubu and The Truth Commission** by Jane Taylor
1998	**Il Ritomo d'Ulisse**
2001	**Zeno at 4am**, libretto by Jane Taylor, score by Kevin Volans
2002	**Confessions**, libretto by Jane Taylor, score by Kevin Volans
	William Kentridge's extensive solo exhibitions include:
1997	Documenta X in Kassel
1998–99	A survey exhibition of his work seen in Brussels, Munich, Barcelona, London, Marseilles and Graz
1999	Museum of Modern Art, New York
1999	Museum of Contemporary Art, San Diego
2001–02	A survey exhibition seen in Washington, New York Chicago, Houston, Los Angeles and Cape Town
1999	Awarded the Carnegie Medal at Carnegie

Robert Lepage

1977	Graduated from the local Conservatoire d' Art in Quebec
1979	**L'attaque quotidienne** by Lepage and Robert Fréchette, Théâtre Hummm, Quebec
1980	**Saturday Night Taxi**, collective collaboration, Théâtre Hummm; **Oomeragh ooh!** by Jean Truss, Grand Théâtre, Quebec
1981	**Jour de pluie** by Gérard Bibeau, Grand Théâtre, Quebec
1982	**Pas d'chicane dans ma cabane**, collective collaboration, Théâtre d'Bon'Humeur, Quebec
1983	**Dieu et l'amour complexe** by Woody Allen, Conservatoire d'Art Dramatique, Quebec
1984	**Solange passe** by Jocelyne Corbeil and Lucie Godbout, Théâtre de la Bordeé
1985	**The Dragons Trilogy**, collective collaboration, Théâtre Repère (winner of nine international awards)
1986	Devised and performed one-man show **Vinci**, Théâtre Repère (winner of three awards)
1987	**Polygraph** by Lepage and Marie Brassard, Théâtre Repère with Cultural Industry and Almeida Theatre, London (winner of two awards)
1988	**Tectonic Plates**, Théâtre Repère with Cultural Industry, Glasgow; **Songe d'une nuit d'eté** by William Shakespeare, Théâtre du Nouveau Monde, Montreal
1989	Appointed Artistic Director of French Theatre at National Arts Centre, Ottawa; **La vie de Galilée** by Brecht, Théâtre du Nouveau Monde, Montreal
1990	**La Visite de la Vielle Dame** by Friedrich Dürenmatt, at National Arts Centre, Ottawa
1991	Created and directed **Needles and Opium**, one-man show, Productions AJP, Montreal (winner of Chalmers Award for Best Canadian Play)
1992	**Bluebeard's Castle** by Bartók and **Ewartung** by Schoenberg, Canadian Opera Company (winner of two awards); **A Midsummer Night's Dream** by Shakespeare, National Theatre, London
1993	Directed and designed Peter Gabriel's **Secret World Tour**; **Macbeth** and **The Tempest** in Japanese, Tokyo
1994	Founding Artistic Director of Ex Machina, Quebec
1995	**The Confessional**, Cinémaginaire, Enigma Films, London and Cinea, France (winner of five awards); **Elsinore**, Ex Machina with Musee d'Art Contemporain, Montreal and partners in France, Berlin, London and Rotterdam
1996	**Polygraph**, adapted from stageplay
1997	**The Geometry of Miracles**, Lepage's contemplation on the works of Frank Lloyd Wright
1998	**The Tempest**, a three-dimensional version, and began working on **Zulu Time**
1999	Began filming John Mighton's **Possible Words**
2000	**The Far Side of The Moon**, a one-man show

Simon McBurney

1957	Born in Cambridge, England
1975	Studied at Cambridge University
1979	Trained at L'École de Mime Jacques Lecoq, Paris
1983	Co-founded **Theatre de Complicite** (now **Complicite**) with Annabel Arden and Marcello Magni
1984	**Put it on Your Head**, a show about the English seaside
1985	**A Minute Too Late**, a smash-hit show about death
1985	**More Bigger Snacks Now** (winner of the Perrier Award)
1986	**Please, Please, Please**, a show about a family at Christmas
1986	**Foodstuff**, a show about eating
1987	**Anything for a Quiet Life**, a show about fear, bureaucracy, Town Halls, committee meetings and despair
1989	**My Army** Parts I and II – one man's account of his experiences with the military in the '50s and '60s
1992	**The Street of Crocodiles**, adapted from stories by Bruno Schulz, Theatre de Complicite/Royal National Theatre co-production, world tour including two West End seasons (awards include L1 Académie Québécoise du Théâtre and Award for Best Foreign Production)
1993	Prudential Arts Award for Theatre; Barcelona Critics 1 Award for Best Foreign Production; and four Laurence Olivier Award nominations
1994	**The Three Lives of Lucie Cabrol**, adapted from the short story by John Berger, world tour between 1994 and 1996 (winner of over ten major international awards including Time Out's Best Theatrical Presentation of 1990s)
1994	**Out of a House Walked a Man**, adapted from the writings of Russian surrealist Daniil Kharms, Theatre de Complicite/Royal National Theatre co-production
1997	**The Caucasian Chalk Circle**, Theatre de Complicite/Royal National Theatre co-production. Winner of Laurence Olivier Award for Best Choreography
1998	**The Chairs**, Theatre de Complicite/Royal Court co-production, West End and Broadway Nominated for six Tony awards including Best Director; a Laurence Olivier nomination; a Time Out Live Award and Barclays/TMA Award for Best Actor
1998	**The Vertical Line**, a multimedia piece with John Berger, performed in the disused Aldwych Tube Station
1999	**Mnemonic**, Salzburg, UK and European tours, London and three-month New York Off-Broadway season (winner of nine awards including Time Out Live Award for Outstanding Achievement and Drama Desk Award for Unique Theatrical Experience)
2000	**Light**, adapted from a book by Swedish writer Torgny Lindgren, UK and European tour
2001	**The Noise of Time**, commissioned by Lincoln Center, New York, a multimedia piece with the Emerson String Quartet, USA and European tours

Yukio Ninagawa

1955	Trained as an actor in a small avant-garde theatre
1967	Established **Gendaijin-Gekijo** (The Contemporary People's Theatre)
1969	**Hearty but Flippant** by Kunio Shimizu, Japan tour
1974	**Romeo and Juliet**, Nissei Theatre, Japan
	He went on to form a partnership with Tadao Nakane and his production company Point Tokyo. Together they have produced **King Lear**, **Oedipus Rex**, **Hamlet**, **Medea**, **Ninagawa Macbeth**, **Suicide for Love**, **Sotoba Komachi** and **Tango at the End of Winter**
1979	**Suicide For Love** won the Grand Prize at the Arts Festival in Japan
1983	**Medea** (first performance) – has since been perfoemed in Greece Italy, France, Canada, UK, USA and Malaysia
1985	**Ninagawa Macbeth**, Edinburgh Festival and Amsterdam
1985	**Medea** and **Ninagawa Macbeth**, the Royal National Theatre, London
1990	**Sotoba Komachi** won Festival Critics Award at Edinburgh Festival
1991	**Tango at the End of Winter**, first production performed in English at the Edinburgh Festival and in London's West End, UK
1991	Awarded an honorary doctorate by Edinburgh University
1992	**The Tempest**, Point Tokyo Company, Japan
1994	**Peer Gynt**, Winter Olympics, Norway
1995	**A Midsummer Night's Dream**, Point Tokyo Company
1996	**A Midsummer Night's Dream**, Mermaid Theatre, London
1997	**Shintoku-Maru** huge success in Tokyo
1999	**King Lear** (Co-production with the Royal Shakespeare Company and Thelma Holt Ltd. With Sainokuni Shakespeare Company, HoriPro and Point Tokyo, starring Nigel Hawthorne)
2000	**The Greeks**, Cocoon Theatre, Tokyo (winner of the Yomiuri Drama Award for Best Director)
2001	**Hearty But Flippant**, Cocoon Theatre, Tokyo, Japan; a revival of his 1969 production
2001	**Macbeth**, a new production produced by HoriPro and the Sainokuni Shakespeare Company, Japan
2001	**Sotoba Komachi** and **Yoroboshi** by Yukio Mishima

Trevor Nunn

1958	Studied at Downing College, Cambridge
1962	Won an ABC Directors Scholarship to the Belgrade Theatre, Coventry
1964	Joined Royal Shakespeare Company, Stratford-upon-Avon
1965	Made Associate Director of the Royal Shakespeare Company
1968	Became the youngest ever Artistic Director of the Royal Shakespeare Company
	Productions at the Royal Shakespeare Company include: **The Ravenger's Tragedy**, **The Relapse**, **The Alchemist**, **Henry V**, **The Taming of the Shrew**, **King Lear**, **Much Ado About Nothing**, **The Winter's Tale**, **HenryVIII**, **Hamlet**, **Macbeth**, **Antony and Cleopatra**, **Coriolanus**, **Julius Caesar**, **Titus Andronicus**, **Romeo and Juliet**, **The Comedy of Errors**, **As You Like It**, **All's Well that Ends Well**, **Once in a Lifetime**, **Three Sisters**, **Juno and the Paycock**, **Othello**, **Blue Angel** and **Measure for Measure**. With his colleague John Caird he co-directed **Nicholas Nickleby** (winner of five Tony Awards), J. M. Barrie's **Peter Pan** and **Les Misérables** (winner of eight Tony Awards)
1982	Opened the Royal Shakespeare Company's new London Home, The Barbican Theatre, with his production of **Henry IV** parts 1 and 2
1986	Opened the Swan Theatre in Stratford-upon-Avon which he conceived
1986	Relinquished his post as Artistic Director of Royal Shakespeare Company
1993	**Arcadia** by Tom Stoppard, the Royal National Theatre, London
1997	He became Artistic Director of Royal National Theatre
1997	**An Enemy of The People** by Henrik Ibsen, Royal National Theatre
1997	**Mutability** by Frank McGuinness, Royal National Theatre
1998	**Not About Nightingales** by Tenessee Williams, Royal National Theatre
1998	**Oklahoma** by Rodgers & Hammerstein, Royal National Theatre (winner of an Emmy Award)
1998	**Betrayal** by Harold Pinter, Royal National Theatre
1999	**The Merchant of Venice** by William Shakespeare, Royal National Theatre
1999	**Summerfolk** by Maxim Gorky, new version by Nick Dear (winner of the South Bank Award for Theatre 1999)
1999	Won 1999 Evening Standard Award and Critics Circle Awards for Best Director for **The Merchant of Venice** and **Summerfolk**
2000	**The Cherry Orchard** by Anton Chekov, new version by David Lan, Royal National Theatre
2000	**In Exremis** by Neil Bartlett, Royal National Theatre
2001	**My Fair Lady** by Lerner & Lowe, Royal National Theatre, transferred to the Theatre Royal, London
2001	**The Relapse** by John Vanbrugh, directed with Stephen Rayne, Royal National Theatre
2001	**South Pacific** by Rodgers & Hammerstein, Royal National Theatre
2002	Relinquished post at the Royal National Theatre

Peter Stein

1964	Moved with Dieter Giesung to Munich Kammerspiele, where he did some freelance dramaturgical work before becoming full-time dramaturg and assistant director
1967	Debut production of **Saved** by Edward Bond
1967	**Love and Intrigue** with actors Jutta Lampe, Edith Clever, Michael Konig and Bruno Ganz who were to form the core of his company
1968	**In the Jungle of the Cities** by Bertolt Brecht; first show with long-time collaborator designer Karl Ernst Herrman
1969	**Torquato Tasso** by Goethe
1969	**Vietnam-Discourse** by Peter Weiss, co-directed with Wolfgang Schwiedrzik
1969	**Early Morning** by Edward Bond at Schauspielhaus, Zurich, Germany
1970	Funded to form a company at the West Berlin Schaubuhne am Halleschen Ufer, Germany
1970	**The Mother** by Brecht
1971	**Peer Gynt** by Henrik Ibsen
1972	**Optimistic Tragedy** by Vsevelod Vishnevsky
1972	**Prinz Friedrich von Homburg** by Heinrich von Kleist, Schaubuhne am Halleschen Ufer, West Berlin
1972	**Purgatory in Inglostadt** by Marieluise Fliesser, Schaubuhne am Halleschen Ufer, West Berlin
1973	**The Piggy Bank**
1974	**Summerfolk** by Gorky; first foreign language production invited to the Royal National Theatre, London
1974	**They Are Dying Out There** by Peter Handke, Schaubuhne am Halleschen Ufer, West Berlin
1976	**The Ring** by Wagner, Paris Opera, France
1978	**Trilogy of Return** and **Great and Small** by Stein's dramaturg Botho Stauss
1984	**The Park** by Botho Stauss
1977	**As You Like It** by William Shakespeare
1981	**Class Enemy** by Nigel Williams, Schaubuhne am Halleschen Ufer, West Berlin
1984	**The Three Sisters** by Anton Chekov
1985	Left the Schaubuhne
1986	**Otello** at the Welsh National Opera, UK
1988	**Falstaff** at Welsh National Opera, UK
1989	**Titus Andronicus** by William Shakespeare, Teatro Ateneo, Rome, Italy
1989	**The Cherry Orchard** by Anton Chekov, Schaubuhne am Halleschen Ufer, West Berlin
1990	**Roberto Zucco** by Bernard-Marie Koltes, Schaubuhne am Halleschen Ufer, West Berlin
1991	Became Director of Theatre Programming at the Salzburg Festival, Austria
1992	**Julius Caesar** with a cast of 32 and 200 extras
1992	**Pelleas et Melisande** with conductor Pierre Boulez at Welsh National Opera
1994	Reworking of his 1980 Schaubuhne production of Aeschylus' **Orestaia** with the Moscow Army Theatre, Russia
1994	**Antony and Cleopatra** by William Shakespeare, Salzburg Festival, Austria

Stein has received numerous awards including *Commandeur de l'Ordre des Arts et Lettres* and *Chevalier de la Legion d'Honneur*, 1992, and the Erasmus Prize,1993.

Habib Tanvir

1940	Laurie Municipal High School, Raipur, India
1944	Morris College, Nagpur
1945	Aligarh Muslim University
1948–50	Editor *Box Office*, a Bombay film weekly
1945–52	Acted in eight feature films; wrote songs and dialogues for films in Bombay
1946–53	Actor-director Indian People's Theatre Association, Bombay
1954	Founded the first professional theatre in India at Delhi, the Hindustani Theatre
1955	Trained in acting at the Royal Academy of Dramatic Art in London
1956–58	Observed theatres in Europe
1959	Founded Naya Theatre
	Productions include: **Mitti Ki Gadi**; **Agra Bazar**; **Charan the Thief**; **Gaon Ka Naam Sasural**; **Bahadur Kalarin**; **Dekh Rahey Hain Nain**; **Basant Ritu Ka Sapna (A Midsummer Night's Dream)**; **Uttar Ram Charitra**; **Mudra Raksha**; **Hirma Ki amar Kahani**; **Sajapur Ki Shanti Bai (The Good Person of Setzuan)**; **Veni Samhar**; **Shatranj Ke Mohrey**; **Merey Baad**
1962–63	Went on a theatre observation tour of the USA sponsored by the Institute of International Education, New York
1964–72	Drama critic for *The Statesman*, *Patriot*, *Link* and *Mainstream*, Delhi, and film critic for *Patriot* and *Link*
1969	Delhi Sangeet Natak Academy Drama Award
1973	MP Govt. Bhopal Award for Drama
1972–78	Nominated Member of Parliament
1982	Fringe First Award for his play **Charan Das Chor** at the Edinburgh Festival
1982	D. Lit. Indian Music at the University of Khairagarh, India
1982	National Award Delhi Padma Shree
1983	Academy of Arts and Literature Award, Delhi
1985	Nandikar Award for Drama, Calcutta
1990	Kalidas Drama Award, Bhopal
2000	Maharashtra State Urdu Academy Award Mumbai for plays and poetry
2001	Aditya Vikram Birla Kala Shikhar Award Mumbai for theatre
2002	Hindi Sahitra Sangh Bhavabhuti Award Bhopal for literature
2002	National Award Padma Bhushan Delhi

Julie Taymor

1974	**Way of Snow**, Arc Theater, New York, International Puppet Festival Washington (previously produced in Java and Bali)
1978	**Tirai**, La MaMa, New York (previously produced in Java, Sumatra and Bali)
1980	**The Haggadah**, New York Shakespeare Festival, PBS Television, 1981
1981	**Black Elk Lives**, Entermedia Theater, New York
1982	**Savages**, Centre Stage, Baltimore
1984	**The King Stag**, American Repertory Theater, Massachusetts; toured Europe, Japan, USA
1985	**Liberty's Taken**, Castle Hill Festival, Massachusetts
1986	**The Transposed Heads**, American Music Theater, Philadelphia, and Lincoln Center, New York
	The Tempest, Theatre for a New Audience at Classic Stage Company, New York
1988	**The Taming of the Shew**, Theatre for a New Audience at Classic Stage Company, New York
	Juan Darién: A Carnival Mass, Music Theater Group, New York; toured to Edinburgh, Little Montreal, Jerusalem, San Francisco (1990–1), Lincoln Centre, New York (1996)
1992	Film **Fool's Fire**, American Playhouse/Rebo Studio/Line Productions/Kerry Orent. Premièred at Sundance Film Festival, USA
	Oedipus Rex, Saito Kinen Festival, Matsumoto, Japan, (Film premièred at Sundance Film Festival, 1993)
1993	**The Magic Flute**, Maggio Musicale, Florence and Turin
1994	**Titus Andronicus**, Theatre for a New Audience, New York
1995	**Salome**, Passiontheater, Germany; Mariinsky Theatre, St Petersburg
	The Flying Dutchman, Los Angeles Opera
1996	**The Green Bird**, Theatre for a New Audience at New Victory Theater, New York, LaJolla Playhouse, California
1998	**The Lion King**, New Amsterdam Theater, New York
2000	Film **Titus**, Clear Blue Sky Productions, Urania Pictures, Overseas Filmgroup

Robert Wilson

1958	Cured of a speech impediment by dancer, Mrs Byrd Hoffman
1959	Educated at University of Texas
1962	Studied painting with George McNeil in Paris
1963	Studied Architecture at Brooklyn's Pratt Institute
1965	Moved to New York
1968	Gathered group of artists and formed The Byrd Hoffman School of Byrds
1969	**The King of Spain** at the Anderson Theatre, New York
1969	**The Life and Times of Sigmund Freud**, Brooklyn Academy of Music
1971	**The Deafman Glance**, a silent opera created in collaboration with Raymond Andrews
1972	**Ka Mountain and Gardenia Terrace** in Shiraz, Iran
1973	**The Life and Times of Joseph Stalin**, a 12-hour silent opera, New York, Europe and South America
1974–75	**A Letter for Queen Victoria** in Europe and New York
1976	**Einstein on the Beach** in collaboration with composer Philip Glass; presented at the Festival d'Avignon, France, and at the Metropolitan Opera House, New York
1979	**Death, Destruction and Detroit** at the Schaubuhne, Berlin
1984	**The Civil Wars**, created with playwright Heiner Muller for the Olympic Arts Festival in Los Angeles but full epic never seen. Individual parts have since been produced in the United States, Europe and Japan
1986	**Alceste**, adapted from Euripides, created with performance artist Laurie Anderson
1987	**Quartet**, created with Heiner Muller
1987	**Death, Destruction and Detroit II**, at the Schaubuhne, Berlin
1988	**Cosmopolitan Greetings**, created with poet Allen Ginsberg
1991	**The Black Rider**, created with singer/songwriter Tom Waits, Thalia Theatre, Hamburg (winner of the German Critics Award)
1991	**Parsifal**, by Wagner, Hamburg State Opera
1991	**The Magic Flute** by Mozart at Opera Bastille, Paris
1991	**Lohengrin**, opera by Wagner at Zurich Opera
1991	**When We Dead Awaken** adapted from Henrik Ibsen
1991/1996	**La Maladie de la Mort** adapted from Marguerite Duras
1992	**Doctor Faustus Lights the Lights** adapted from Gertrude Stein (winner of two Italian Premio Ubu Awards)
1993	**Alice in Bed** created with writer Susan Sontag, Thalia Theatre, Hamburg
1993–97	**Madame Butterfly** by Puccini, Opera Bastille, Paris
1996	**Time Rocker** created with singer/songwriter Lou Reed, Thalia Theatre, Hamburg
1996	**Four Saints in Three Acts** adapted from Gertrude Stein
2000	**POE-try** created with Lou Reed at Thalia Theatre, Hamburg

Wilson is recipient of two Rockefellar and two Guggenheim fellowships. He has been named a Lion of the Performing Arts by the New York Public Library and Texas Artist of the Year by the Art League, Houston. He has received an Institute Honor from The American Institute of Architects, an honorary doctorate from the Pratt Institute, a Bessie Award, an Obie Award for Direction, A Drama Desk Award for Lifetime Achievement in 1996, and the Harvard Excellence in Design Award, 1998.

Arena theatre: The acting area is totally surrounded by the audience (theatre-in-the-round). This enables a greater number of seats to be nearer the action and therefore a closer relationship between audience and actors.

Back lit: When actors or objects are behind a gauze or similar piece of thin material they cannot be seen until a light is shone on them from behind. The audience can then see the action naturalistically or as shadow effects according to the angle of the lighting.

Brecht: Bertolt Brecht (1898–1956) was a German dramatist, poet, director and theoretician, who developed the notion of 'epic' theatre and the theory of alienation, which allows the audience sufficient distance from the emotional entanglement of a story to intellectually respond to the play.

Bunraku: A Japanese form of puppet theatre in which puppets are usually about four-feet high, with moving features as well as limbs. Each puppet is manipulated by up to three puppeteers who remain onstage.

Casting: Used to describe the process of choosing and contracting actors to play a specific role in a show.

Costume designer: The costume designer works with the director and set designer to create the desired dress for each actor and performer. This can also include wigs and makeup in some cases. The final designs for each costume, can either be made in the wardrobe department or hired.

Director: The director is responsible for the artistic vision and eventual staging of a production. The role of director is historically fairly new. It was always the leading actor who had the final say in polishing a production while the stage manager was responsible for casting and coordinating the set and costumes etc. The first director to be credited in a programme was in the 1820s, and the role had become more familiar by the 1870s, although it was still taken by someone involved in the show – writer, actor or stage manager. The first person in Britain to be exclusively a director was Lewis Wingfield who directed Lily Langtry in **As You Like It** in 1890. Internationally the role was developing at varying degrees; the Duke of Saxemeiningen was a great influence to the likes of Stanislavski, Reindhart and Antione. Theorists such as Edward Gordon Craig and Appia helped to elevate the role to that of the main figurehead which began the move towards 'directors theatre' as it is sometimes labeled today.

Games: Some directors use games in rehearsals to warm up the actors both mentally and physically, and to encourage response, reflex, concentration and company collaboration.

German Expressionism: Theatrical movement dominating German theatre in 1920s. Inspired by many influences including Strindberg and Dadaism, the result was a theatre in which extreme psychological states were obsessively explored with bold symbolic settings and costumes. Later Expressionists were Toller, Capek and Elmer Rice.

Improvisation: A rehearsal or performance method where the actors work without a script, making up their own words or visual score based on a given circumstance or theme.

Kabuki theatre: A later (16th-century) form of Japanese Noh plays (see Noh Drama) developed from the puppet theatre. Kabuki dramas are performed on a wide shallow stage with a built-up runway on which the actors enter. The staging uses elaborate scenery, costumes, and makeup. Female roles are played by male actors who train from a young age.

Lecoq: Jacques Lecoq, founder of L'École de Mime Jacques Lecoq, Paris, an international professional school of mime and theatre based on movement and the human body.

Lighting designer: The lighting designer is responsible for creating the desired effect or mood of each part of the production, according to the director's requirements. The technician responsible for the operation of the lighting for each performance is called the electrician and is stationed at a desk with a view of the acting area either behind or sometimes above the audience.

Mise en scène: This term is used to describe the director's role as visual story teller; how they choose to arrange the objects and scenery that the designer has supplied in order to create the desired environment.

Noh (or Nō) drama: Japanese classical theatre dating from the 14th century, using stylised movement, costumes and makeup. They are performed on a square stage raised slightly from the ground (on which the audience sits on two sides). To one side is a balcony with ten singers and at the back a smaller stage with four musicians and two stage hands. The actors enter along a long slanting walk. There are no sets, just simple frameworks to represent buildings. There are usually only two actors. The whole entertainment lasts about seven hours.

Pantomime: In the UK the contemporary meaning for pantomime is a lighthearted, elaborate Christmas show, with plenty of audience participation, songs, big frocks and silly gags. The stories are usually based on fairytales and traditionally the principal boy is played by a woman and the dame is played by a man. Pantomime also means an entertainment in Rome given by one actor with a compartmented mask playing several roles. The term was also used for 18th-century mythical ballets, mime plays and dumb-show melodramas.

Producer: The organisation of a production from concept to closing is handled by the producer, or a production group, according to the scale of the production. They do everything from raising the initial funding to financial and administrative control throughout the whole production.

Props: This term is used for all the objects used in a show; cups, saucers, umbrellas, etc. They are the responsibility of the stage manager who sets them on stage before the show begins and lays out props that need to be brought on by an actor on a props table backstage. Props like watches or pens or money that the actor might carry in their costume are called personal props.

Proscenium theatre: Proscenium staging is a conventional form, also known as 'end stage' or 'end on', with the seating in rows facing an arched platform. The acting area can be blanked off from the audience's view by a curtain which either raises or parts when the action is about to start. The arch is usually surrounded by highly decorative molding, hence 'picture-frame stage'. The set invariably represents three sides of a room, the curtained opening being known as 'the fourth wall'.

Rehearsal: The rehearsal period is the intensive time the director spends with the company creating the show. It can last from three weeks upwards depending on culture and finances. The show will be taken straight from the rehearsal process into the theatre where it will go into a technical rehearsal on the stage (see technical rehearsal).

Set: This term is used to describe the entire environment designed by the set designer on which the show takes place. It includes the built construction of walls, back drops, etc. plus the space, flooring, furniture and props.

Set designer: The set designer works in close conjunction with the director to determine the visual aspect of the production. They design the scenery and often the costumes as well. They work closely with the production manager to ensure that the budget is maintained and the set is delivered.

Sound designer: Sound design can vary from a few basic sound effects to elaborate atmospheric aural creations. This may also include music in whatever form is required for a specific production. The operation of the equipment relaying the sound for each performance is by a sound technician at a desk usually adjacent to the lighting desk.

Stage manager: The stage manager works with a team of assistants and is responsible for staging the production to the director's requirements. This includes coordinating everyone involved in the production from day one of rehearsal to the running of the show during performances.

Stanislavski: Konstantin Stanislavski (1863–1938), a Russian actor, director and co-founder of the Moscow Art Theatre. His universally renowned theory on acting – instructing the actor to find the truth within himself about the character he is playing – is still the basis for most professional acting training today.

Technical rehearsal: These follow the rehearsal process and last from two days to several weeks depending on the size of the show. It is here that all the elements that the director has been overseeing – actors, set, costumes, lights, sound – come together and are made to work in situ. During the 'technical' the stage manager runs the rehearsal in close contact with the director and every technical moment of the show is made to work to perfection before moving on. The actors cut their speech to move from cue to cue and will occasionally walk the space for the director and lighting designer to examine the lighting.

Thrust stage: The thrust is when part, usually the centre, of the main acting area projects into the audience like an apron. When used with arena theatre a segment of the circle forms the main acting area from which the thrust projects so that the audience is on three sides. This type of staging, in varying forms, was used by ancient Greek theatre, and both Eastern and Western classical theatre right up to today.

172 INDEX

p2 **Confessions of Zeno**, Dawid Minnaar, photograph by Ruphin Coudyzer; p10 **Rooms in the Emperor's Palace**, Julia Varley, photograph by Tony d'Urso; pp12–13 **Judith**, (1–2) photograph by Torben Huss, (3) by Fiora Bemporad; pp14–15 **Rooms in the Emperor's Palace**, (1) photograph by Tony d'Urso, (2) by Paul Östergård, (3–4) by Tony d'Urso; p16 **Ode to Progress**, (1) photograph by Tony d'Urso, (2–4) courtesy Odin Teatret; p18 **Ode to Progress**, photograph by Jan Rüsz; p19 **Kaosmos**, courtesy Odin Teatret; pp20–21 **Mythos** (1) poster by Marco Donati, (2) photograph by Tony d'Urso; p22 **Miss Julie**, courtesy the SITI Company; pp24–25 (1–5) courtesy the SITI Company; p26 **Score**, (1–2) courtesy the SITI Company; p27 **Small Lives/Big Dreams**, (3) courtesy the SITI Company; pp28–29 **Once in a Lifetime**, (1–3) photographs by Richard Feldman; p30 **The Medium** (1) photograph by Joan Marcus, **Bob** (2) photograph by Joan Marcus; p31 **War of the Worlds**, (3) photograph by John Nati; p32 **Cabin Pressure**, (1) courtesy the SITI Company, **Private Lives**, (2) courtesy the SITI Company; p33 **Going, Going, Gone**, (3) courtesy the SITI Company; p34 **As You Like It**, Scott Handy as Orlando and Adrian Lester as Rosalind, courtesy Cheek By Jowl; p36 **Boris Godunuv**, (1–2) courtesy Cheek By Jowl; p37 **Le Cid**, photograph by Philippe Delacroix; pp38–39 **Homebody/Kabul**, (1–5) photographs by Keith Pattison; p40 **The Winter's Tale**, (1) photograph by Geraint Lewis; p41 (2) Nick Ormerod and Declan Donnellan, photograph by Simon Annand; p42 **Lady Betty**, (1) photograph by John Haynes; p43 **The Duchess of Malfi**, (2) courtesy Cheek By Jowl; p44 **Fuente Ovejuna**, (1) photograph by John Haynes; p45 **Angels in America Part 1: Millennium Approaches**, (2) photograph by John Haynes; p46 **Ubu and the Truth Commission**, courtesy William Kentridge; pp48–49 **Ubu and the Truth Commission**, (1–2) courtesy William Kentridge, (3) photograph by Ruphin Coudyzer; pp50–51 **Ubu tells the Truth**, (1–4) courtesy William Kentridge, **Ubu and the Truth Commission**, (5) courtesy William Kentridge; pp52–53 **Il Ritorno d'Ulisse**, (1) photograph by Andrew McIlleron, (2–3) courtesy William Kentridge; pp54–55 **Confessions of Zeno**, (1) courtesy William Kentridge, (2) photograph by Ruphin Coudyzer, (3–4) courtesy William Kentridge; pp56–57 **Faustus in Africa!**, (1) courtesy William Kentridge, (2) photograph by Ruphin Coudyzer, (3) courtesy William Kentridge; pp58–59 **Faustus in Africa!**, photograph by Pascal Maine; p60 **Elsinor**, photograph by Emmanuel Valette; pp62–63 **The Far Side of the Moon**, (1) photograph by Cylla Von Tiedemann, (2–3) photographs by Sophie Grenier; pp64–65 **Coriolanus** (1) photograph by Emmanuel Valette, **Macbeth** (2) photograph by Emmanuel Valette, **The Tempest** (3–5) photographs by Emmanuel Valette; pp66–67 **A Midsummer Night's Dream**, (1–2) photographs by Neil Libbert; pp68–71 **Elsinor**, (1) photograph by Richard Max Tremblay, (2–3) photographs by Donald Cooper, (4) photograph by Emmanuel Valette, (5) photograph by Richard Max Tremblay; p72 **The Noise of Time**, photograph by Joan Marcus; pp74–75 **Out of a House Walked a Man...**, (1–2) photographs by Nobby Clark; p76 **The Street of Crocodiles**, (1) photograph by Nobby Clarke; p77 **The Three Lives of Lucie Cabrol**, (2–3) photographs by Simon Annand; p78 **Mnemonic**, photograph by Sebastian Hoppe; pp80–81 **Mnemonic**, photographs by Sarah Anslie; p82–83 **The Chairs**, (1–2) photographs by Sarah Ainslie; pp84–85 **The Visit**, (1–2) photographs by Red Saunders; p86 **Medea**, photograph by Alastair Muir; pp88–89 **Medea**, (1–3) photographs by Alastair Muir; pp90–91 **Hinotori**, (1–5) courtesy Yukio Horio; pp92–93 (1–4), all sketches courtesy Yukio Ninagawa; pp94–97 **King Lear**, courtesy Yukio Horio; p98 **South Pacific**, Edward Baker-Duly and Elaine Tan, photograph by Marilyn Kingwill; p100 **Porgy and Bess**, (1) photograph by Guy Gravett; p101 **Macbeth**, (2–3) photograph by Joe Cocks; pp102–103 Nicholas Nickleby, photograph by Reg Wilson; pp104–105 **South Pacific**, (1–2) photographs by Marilyn Kingwill; pp106–107 **Cats**, (1–2) photographs by Alastair Muir; p108 **Faust**, photograph by Ruth Walz; p111 **Anthony and Cleopatra**, (1–2) photographs by Ruth Walz; pp112–113 **Faust**, (1–5) photographs by Ruth Walz; p114 **Orestaia**, (1–2) photographs by Ruth Walz; p115 **Hamlet**, (3) photograph by Ruth Walz; pp116–119 **Julius Caesar**, (1–3) photographs by Ruth Walz; p120 Actors, courtesy Habib Tanvir; pp122–123 **Charan Das Chor**, (1–3) courtesy Habib Tanvir; p124 **Hirma Ki Amar Kahani**, (1–2) courtesy Habib Tanvir; pp125–127 **Dekh Rahey Hain Nain**, (3–6) courtesy Habib Tanvir; pp128–129 **Bahadur Kalarin**, (1–3) courtesy Habib Tanvir; pp130–131 **Bahadur Kalarin**, (1–5) courtesy Habib Tanvir; pp132–133 **Basant Ritu Ka Sapna**, (1–5) courtesy Habib Tanvir; p134 **Fool's Fire**, photograph by Richard Feldman; pp136–137 **The Tempest**, (1–2) photograph by Richard Feldman; pp138–139 **The King Stag**, (1–6) courtesy Julie Taymor, (7–8) photographs by Richard Feldman; pp140–141 **Juan Darién: A Carnival Mass**, (1) courtesy Julie Taymor, (2) photograph by Richard Feldman; pp142–143 **Juan Darién: A Carnival Mass**, (1) photograph by Richard Feldman, (2–4) courtesy Julie Taymor; pp144–145 **Fool's Fire**, (1) courtesy Julie Taymor, (2) photograph by Richard Feldman; pp146–147 **The Lion King**, (1–3) courtesy Julie Taymor, © Disney Enterprises, Inc.; p148 **Frida**, (1–3) courtesy Miramax, 2002, **Titus**, (4) photograph by Alessia Bulgari; p149 **Oedipus Rex**, (3) photograph by Akira Kinoshita; p150 **Orlando**, Jutte Lampe, courtesy Robert Wilson; pp152–153 **The Deafman Glance**, (1–2) photographs by Martin Bough; pp154–155 **Death, Destruction and Detroit III**, photograph by Tilde de Tullio; p156 **The Black Rider**, (1) photograph by Marie-Noelle Robert; p157 **Alceste**, (2–3) courtesy Robert Wilson; pp158–159 **O Corvo Branco (White Raven)**, (4) photograph by Javier del Real; p161 **The Magic Flute**, (1) photograph by Peter Perazio, **King Lear**, (2) courtesy Robert Wilson; p162 **Memory Loss**, (1) courtesy Robert Wilson, **Bluebeard's Castle**, (2) courtesy Robert Wilson, **The CIVIL warS**, (3) photographer Richard Feldman, **Einstein on the Beach**, (4) courtesy Robert Wilson; p163 **Ka Mountain and Gardenia Terrace**, (5) courtesy Robert Wilson; p164 Eugenio Barba, photograph by Fiora Bemporad, Anne Bogart, courtesy the SITI Company; p165 Declan Donnellan, courtesy Cheek By Jowl, William Kentridge, photograph by Lori Waselchuk; p166 Robert Lepage, photograph by Cylla Von Tiedemann, Simon McBurney, photograph by Sarah Anslie; 166 Yukio Ninagawa, photograph by Alastair Muir, Trevor Nunn, photograph by Guy Gravett; p167 Peter Stein, photograph by Ruth Walz; p168 Julie Taymor, courtesy Chris Kanarick, Robert Wilson, courtesy Aaron Beebe; p175 **Elsinor**, Robert Lepage, photograph by Emmanuelle Valette.

176

PICTURE CREDITS